T0365652

Inside a Poet's Heart

AKEAM SIMMONS

iUniverse LLC
Bloomington

INSIDE A POET'S HEART

iUniverse books may be ordered through booksellers or by contacting:

iUniverse LLC
1663 Liberty Drive
Bloomington, IN 47403
www.iuniverse.com
1-800-Authors (1-800-288-4677)

ISBN: 978-1-4917-1706-6 (sc)
ISBN: 978-1-4917-1707-3 (e)

Printed in the United States of America.

iUniverse rev. date: 11/22/2013

Contents

To the all enveloping God, that shaped and holds the whole universe in his hand, that envelopes my past, my present, and molds my future-whose very breath ensues from my nostrils, so to keep me fresh with life every day, and empowers my every moment with new seeds from him!!

To the Lady of my dreams that my heart longs for, my soul yearns for, and my flesh burns for with unyielding passions delight. Oh that I might hide my heart within the secret chambers of her heart. Nightly, I hastened to sleep, for soon she comes to me with kisses so sweet—My wife, my lover, my friend, my princess that turns my midnights into fresh early mornings; my sweetie that helped me to live again when I had but died.

To my mother, of whom I will always love and carry in my heart; I now know that some things you can never get over, you just learn to live with them . . . .

Bernice Potter—1941-2013

But A Soul

Swim the ocean, and you feel the depth of me
Glide the sky and reach the heavens,
and you feel the breath of me
Go beyond the farthest star, and you feel the height of me
Number the sands of the sea, and you feel the measure of me

I am but a soul

The earth and the sky are my brothers
The very winds that carry the fouls are my breaths
The Marking bird sings of me
The Canary sings to me
And the Eagle follows me

I am but a soul

I am more precious than gold
More endearing than diamond
More usable than coal
And more plenteous than dirt itself

I am but a soul

I am the emotions of all
Yet conclusively I am THE ONE
I am filled with splendor, and joy, and
happiness, and sorrow, all at once
I am the ending at the beginning, and
the beginning at the ending
I am never at rest, for I move continuously upon earth's crest

I am but a soul

I give sound to the ear
Without me the earth is but silence
I give sight to the eye
Without me there be nothing to see
I give reason to the mind
Thought is but my projected motives

I am but a soul

I am your love and your lover
I am the one that helps you make it through your nights
I help you carry your burdens
I lighten your heavy loads

I am the rain after your drought
I am the sun after your winter
I am your very blossoming rose with no prickly thorns
I am your hope for tomorrow and your joy in sorrow

I am but a soul

There is no you without me
Acknowledge me
Embrace me
Grow with me
And the earth becomes your heaven, and
the sky becomes your endless treasure

I am but a soul . . . . YOUR SOUL

Wounded Fool

I've faltered
My heart is fleeting beating sluggishly

I hold my hand over this heart of flesh
And hope and pray nobody see the broken me

What's I am to do when I know that's all I can do
And still I hurt deeply

My hands are empty
My heart is bleeding
My eyes shower with yesterday's tears

I am but a fool
For only fools break their own heart over and over again
Only a fool does not learn from yesterday

I tell myself next time
And next time I say but next time
Oh what folly to never learn from past mistakes

It is a pity to look upon a broken one
Who is doing the best they can
To stand, but falls anyhow

My trusted friend who pierced me through,
and through, and through
Then vanished while I licked my wounds

But I'll be alright
I always do pick up the pieces of my broken shattered heart
And hold them together until they mend again

And I promise myself I won't be a fool again
Next time

Supernatural

Awake oh burning sun
For my work is not nearly done
Oh shine; oh shine until I am all spun
Then I'll know my race is won

Stand still thou glowing moon
Thou lonely night
That glitters so bright
And disturb even the midnight
Lone me thy glowing light
So I may find my sight
To walk in all my Father's might

Oh twinkle twinkle little star
That cast your light from afar
Touch my life if but ajar
As I rage this holy war

Oh wind, oh wind that sings so sweet
When I tarry too long please push my feet
No matter how heavy the load or difficult the feat
Blow on me and push me to meet
My savior on those golden streets

Oh rain, oh rain, rain upon me
And fill my soul the inner sea
And wash this filth, this vile from the me that only I see
Let my cup run over and over again
until I see the Master's key
And fall on my knee
For creating the whole of me

Heart Break

My love, my love is now gone
Cause my lover has deserted and left home
Like melting ice cream without a cone
I be formlessly filled with fear walking now in life alone

My days are nights and my nights are ravenous
midnights while walking alone
Oh how I miss my loves touch—that early morning moan
My heart cries and weeps and hope that
soon you'll come back home
Or shall I wait and hope that of you God made a clone

It is hard to carry on when no one loves you

My days are filled with prayers to find
strength just to carry on
Like a starving dog chewing on a withered dry bone
Hoping to find nourishment from
something that's now gone
Oh what pain, what misery, to know
now some other feels your zone

My heart heavy, my soul empty, my
mind reaps of you leaving home
Leaping to another's arms to call home
Down lonely avenues of sacred streets I roam
Passionately seeking a new love that can atone
And save me from this suicidal loneliness
and isolation that I now prone

Please, please, oh Father pierce through this
heartache that causes me to moan
And steals my joy and happiness because of a broken home

I continue to preach to myself of a love that is now gone
Of how I can make it through this even walking alone
Where my lover's love is now withdrawn
And given to another for happily moans

A broken heart still hurts even when you're fully grown
Realizing some other dips from my
lover's well for happy tones
My mind now awfully blown
It is hard to move on when nobody loves
you, and no love I am shown

I close my eyes for sleep hoping when
I awake I'll be not alone
I want to plead for my lover to come back home
But I too fear that I cannot get pass
somebody else has drawn
From my love's well that use to be mine alone

So now I pray a little harder, a little longer for God to atone
Before I blast myself, and cast myself to a
place no one wants to call home

Pit Fall

It's so hard to move on
Every day is such a task
And the task be just making it through the day
Shaking the demons that's now drawn to me
Advising demons, lust demons, pity demons, hate demons
All now seek to be friends of mine

Difficulties be trying to live when no one loves you

How do I breathe again when I watched my heart
My heart of yester year
My heart so dear
My heart that once shared my blues
and brought joy to my eyes
My heart that walked away form me
And left me to die and dwell in a living grave

Still I sneak a peak in public
Cause I no longer handle private moments
I ask do you really see what you have done to us
To those that have never been
Now those that will never be

All because of blind eyes
And lustful flesh
And a demon that just wants something
to play with and ravage

I wonder how long will it be
Before all of you is gone
And you become a stranger even to yourself

Will my bed still be empty
Will my heart desire to attempt to bring back the former you

But still I pray for you
I hope that you will be alright with this new you
I have fallen

I have fallen in a pit
A pit that I must not allow myself to get use to
But I will rise again

I must
For I refuse to allow your leaving
To mold me down unwanted evil paths

I cry for you now
Realizing I lost you long ago
Demon in pretty clothes with a silver tongue
A demon whose gold was much bigger than mine
Who built a lie of me that you readily conceived

And though my tears are bitter
And stained with loving thoughts of you
And pain and hurt and deceit

I still love you
I don't want to
But I still love you

Desperately I try to hide my feelings
But I still love you
You are with someone else
But I still love you

Damnnnn

I guess
I am but a fool
Who has fallen in a pit
And don't know how to come out
Or even do I want to

Appreciated

Any man that does not know your worth
Is no doubt still operates under a curse
Whose only desire is your body and what is in your purse
Him you will never wean, you will only be his nurse
And even then he will never put you first

You have forgotten your true beauty so you
circum, not wanting to be alone
And leave your queenship bowing for
only some one else's bone
Under appreciated and little love have you been shown

But never forget that you are a queen
Even when sometimes you have to be mean
And let the dark survival side of you be seen
You are still a queen
And need a king's shoulder to lean

Although you do sometimes carry a load
And men act like something less than a toad
While no red carpet been laid for you, you
must forge down the regal road
Upholding your integrity while abiding by the royal code

All I am is because of you
The king in me always comes through
When I see the queen in you renew
And show me what kings are to do

Down through the years you've helped us survive
And kept the royal seed in me alive
Even when good fortune in me had taken a dive

Sometimes we are but stupid, and can't
see the forest for the trees
And can't express what we truly mean
But still inside we thirst still to be the
shoulder that you come to lean

I need you, we need you dear queen
To always be a queen
And help us childish men grow from
being such grown adolescent teens

Letter To My Child

How deeply it breaks my heart to see
How deeply I have hurt you

Caught up in my own mess, I failed to see
How much I was destroying you
So many issues and emotional baggage
I was ascribing to you

And even though, you are a child
You have been more of an adult than I've been

I see the welts of pain riddle across your face
Pain that I just don't know how to ease or erase
Pain that pains me so deeply
Secretly I cry for you
Of the joy that I stole from you
And forced you to grow up too soon

You acted like an adult while I acted like a child
Why didn't I just leave
It would have hurt you a little first
But you would have soon recovered
because you are strong like that

But . . . . no . . . . no . . . no
I had to stay and rob you of your youth
And present you with a life filled with
hurt and disappointment

I so pray that God will restore
All that you allowed me to tarnish and mar
To restore your bright smile
Your confident look
Your bubbling personality

May God forgive me for the pain that
I have caused you my child

Proverbs

-Every generation produces its own kind
It gives birth to its leaders as well as its peasants

-Ignorance is reserved for the unlearned
But stupidity baths upon all-the learned,
the unlearned, and the fool

-To survive
Man does what he has to do
Even lie to himself

-When man cease to dream
He dies a slow agonizing death

-It is absolutely futile to try to reason with a fool
For they will never see their true
reflection in their mirror of life

-If you're not feeling resistance
You're not moving forward

-The worst prisons are the ones that has no
bars, or locks, or cells, nor guards

-The most precious things in life are free

-A father can have no greater treasure than
of a young granddaughter's eyes
For he is never less than perfect

-If you have to have somebody else to define who you are
Then you are still nobody

-Only a fool speaks his whole mind

-Taste your words before they are uttered
For you can never take them back, or silence
them once they are gone from you

-Step cautiously
For your enemies are always but a few steps away

-Choose your cook very carefully
For that which flows from you are the recipes of your cook

-Nothing is free
Nothing is discounted
Everything has a full price
For the universe demands it to be so

-Spousal faithfulness is like the morning
dew resting upon the blades of grass

-Hold not back your tears
For they contain the hurt that needs to leave you

-Times of adversity will always unveil who is your real enemy

-Man often times want that which he cannot have

-Men fear that for which they do not understand

-Differences frighten ignorant men

-Old age is when you can no longer feel young

-Death is when the ability to dream is lost-

A Prayer

Oh MY Lord; my God; my everlasting Father. I praise you for you are the only wise, true, and almighty God. You leave your majestic heaven to come see about me, and you left an angel to watch over me and keep me in all of my ways. I worship you; I honor your name among the nations.

Lord, give me the strength to endure during my times of trouble. Let me not be consumed by my enemies; give me the wisdom to fight with love, compassion, and faith; and when I become weary, give me the strength to fight on.

Soaring

You lay quietly amidst the still clouds
in the never ending blue sky
Fearless, faceless, formless, but full of depth and I know why
Easing ever so slowly as men below pass by
Always wanting, waiting for the clouds to cry

Oh touch me now you that is ever so nigh
And fill my mind with wonders before I die
To feel the joy of how birds do soar and fly

Pierce me through that I'll not lie
As the fowls of the living that's only good to fry

Unfulfilled, misery and hurt caused me to sigh
And quiet desperation caused me to silently cry
While unappreciated toiling gifts made me shy

But I am still a conqueror for my Father does not lie
So I shout to all of my enemies of defeat good bye
And walk in victory every day of my life

Sometimes in the rain the colorful bird fly
Perhaps sometimes to hide the tears that he often cry
But he will laugh and laugh as soon as he dry

For he is always living to rule the sky
Every storm pushes him to rise ever so high
To flee those that are afraid of storms or even to try and fly

Proverbs

-From the lips of anger
Shoots forth arrows of unrestrained truth

-Some women only want
A husband that is simply an upgraded son

-Some men only want
A wife who is simply a maid

-To live on earth and not expect some storms is foolishness
To walk in the foot steps of manhood and
expect no troubles is great foolishness

-To capture a true lover
You must first set them free

-The Past and the Future meet at the Present

-Sex is but a slave master

-Drink not the nectar of sexual pleasure
And you will never leave the wife of your youth

-You never see the real man until power is thrust upon him
For power never changes a man, it
simply reveals his true self

-The love of money accelerates the folly of fools

-You cannot miss that which you cannot measure
And you cannot savor that which you've never had

Hope

My friend looks at me through eyes of hate
Never was there a friend who did not betray
My cup spills over
Yet I thirst all the day long
I am weary about tomorrow
For I know not what it shall bring
But yet
I long for tomorrow
For my change must be in the hymnals of tomorrow

My breastplate fails me
For my heart bleeds from piercing through
Sleep is a sweet nectar that gives me moments of refuge
From my storms

Wrath is the choice of fools
So I desperately seek to face my enemies
And run through my storms with a degree of bold calmness

The Lord will not suffer me to be moved
Though my strength wavers
I shall not be moved
I shall overcome and be better than ever

My enemies and my storms
Simply force me to be stronger
In my weakness
I am made strong

I become whole
After being broken
And my cup overflows after being emptied

Longing For Love

I sit numbered in a crowd full of despair
Longing for kindled love for two to share
To drive away the loneliness with heart felt care
Where two become one in loves declare

I long for your warm embrace
Your gentle touch your elegant grace
Your beauty that shines brightly upon my face
That causes my heart to leap and race

All of life I have waited for a love so pure
To still all the hurt and pains I had to endure
Hoping and waiting for my lover to come and cure
And help my wholeness become so sure

I wait to dance the night away
In the arms of one whose heart will never stray
And whose love will always be true
and faithful come what may

Oh love, my lover that walks in the light of day
And change my tears of loneliness
into cool waters of the bay
You turn my midnights into the sweetest day

Though time is not on my side
I'll still wait and hope with you to ride
Through hymnals of time where only love can guild
Beyond dark clouds where you and my heart abide

Oh that I might leave this valley and climb to the mountain
Where peaks of splendor is certain
And where my feeling of love be not burdened

My Family Lives In Me

I don't represent, but I present
My family unto the world
For all of my family lives through me
All of my experiences are extracted from them

I am them through and through
My ancestors who were slaves bound by chains
Dwell in me
For that is the unexplainable reason
Why I fail to trust in any man
Particularly those whose skin is for lighter than mine

I fight that innate subservient attitude
Towards the white man
Given me by my great grand daddy
Who spent his entire life as a white man's commodity

I watched my daddy
Beat my mama like another man
So now it pains me
Even the very thought of hitting a woman
My mama ruled my daddy
My grand mama ruled my grand daddy
Now I fight the feeling of wanting a woman to rule me

Yes
They unwittingly created me
All of me
Even the dark side of me

And without even trying
The formulation continues
I see my grand mother in my daughters
And my father's temper in my sons
And I know too
That they shall have some me

I see me
In my grand baby
I smile because I know
That the wise me dwell in them
Then I lower my head
For I know too that the me
Before wisdom took hold of me
The me who was foolish
Rested in my children too

I can only pass on
Who I am
And most of that
Was given to me from my father's father

So I present to the world
My family
All of them
From Africa to North America
I be them
All of my family is in me

The Ten Thousand Things

I am in all things
And all things are in me
I am part of everything
And everything is a part of me

I am the past
I am the present
I am the future

There is no increasing me
And no diminishing me
I am the whole of all things

I only change from one form to another
That which the blind call death
Is merely a change
A reconfiguration of molecules that this live
An extension of the ten thousand things

I evolve
I revolve
Because there was a Then
There is a now
And because there is a Now
There is a Will Be

My foot is already thrust in the sands of time
Never to be moved
Only to be shifted
To be changed

My mind is eternal
Though the mountains break apart
And the sands blow away
I shall not be moved

Though the winds blow away
And the clouds disappear
I shall not be moved
Though the sun becomes dark
And the moon runs away
I shall not be moved

For I am of the ten thousand things
The whole of nature
The sky
The sun
The stars
The trees
The dirt
The ocean

I am of the ten thousand things
That connect the whole of the universe
I am of the ten thousand things
That are of the ten thousand things
That are of the ten thousand things

Whatever your eyes behold
You see a glimpse of me
For I am part of the whole
Of the ten thousand things

Hope Of Love

In the darkness I watch the shadows of the sloping trees
And are captivated by what possibly could be for me
Through the darkness I still see
A place for me and my lover to be

The night's crickets sings of our love
The stars announce our passion from above
For we are as compatible as a hand in a glove
And as comforting as the song of the Morning dove

Have yet to find you
But still I wait and search as a lover do
Hoping praying that I will perhaps stumble upon you

I skip through fields of daisies
While sweet thoughts of you make me crazy
Staring up at the sky as though lazy

I wait impatiently
Hoping that you will soon come and complete me

Like a raging stormy sea
I am restless shivering of thoughts of what will be
So I wait and wait impatiently
For the other half of me
To come and rescue me from a heart that is too long blue

Good Fear

Only the dead is without fear
Fear is a mechanism designed by God himself
For the survival and preservation of man

It is the fight or run
Vigor thrust inside man's veins

Fear causes his muscles to tighten
His breaths to quicken
His feet to lighten
His strength to increase

Fear warns him
Of pending danger
Or hurt and harm

Fear is more of man's friend
Than his enemy

Brave men fear
Heroes fear
Wise men fear
And even fools fear sometimes

Bravery is performing the task
In-spite of fear
Courage is performing the task even in fear

Fear significance is shown through infants
For they display fear
Before a smile or laughter
Before they learn to walk or talk
Or even to coo

Embrace your fears
Focus your fears
Allow your fears to work for you
And with you
Then you shall become more than a conqueror

What To Do With Madear

Noah stood by old man Ollen's bed side; hands clasp together with his head dropped deeply into the locks of his shoulders. He whispered

Noah had been a pastor for nearly five decades. He had learned to hate sickness, disease, and death. He had seen them steal life from the young and the old; he had witness sickness tare a family apart, and steal the will to live from infants. Even though he despised sickness and a prayer. Old man Ollen lay upon his hospital bed staring blankly up at the ceiling; sheets draped half way on him, and the blue hospital diaper partly exposed to any visitor that might enter the room. His wife sat in any adjacent corner silently weeping. death passionately, he became accustom to them always being around. There is no place, no city, no state, no nation where he could go that sickness, disease, and death was not already there.

Ollen's breaths were short and quick. The hospice nurse eased into the room and stood beside Ollen's bed and gently rubbed his chest. "Mrs. Ollen it won't be long now." She said softly, hardly above a whisper. Gently she squeezed Noah's shoulder as she quietly left the room.

Noah was concern about Mrs. Ollen. All five of their children had preceded them in death. They had been married for over fifty years. She was eighty five years old, and the only family she had was her grandchildren and her church family. He thought that soon Mrs. Ollen would have to got to a place that Noah despised almost as much as death it self-a nursing home. As pastor, Noah hated visiting the nursing homes. He felt that it was a place reserved for those that were waiting to die. When he visited the nursing homes, many patients lined the halls in their wheel chairs-most asleep, some awake, and slumped over in their chairs staring aimlessly at Noah as he passed by them. He certainly hoped that wouldn't be Mrs. Ollen's fate.

Suddenly, Mr. Ollen exhaled hard, and then stopped breathing. Mrs. Ollen leaped to her feet, leaned over and held Mr. Ollen as she spoke amidst a torrent of sobs. "Ohhhh, don't leave me honey; you can't . . . . You just can't. Oh God please don't take him." She wept hard as she pounded Mr. Ollen's chest.

A lonely tear drop eased down Noah's cheek. Although he had witness this seen hundreds of times, he still wasn't at ease with it. He always hurt right along with the family.

"He's in a better place now sister Ollen. Now you've got to take care of yourself."

"There is no me without Ollen pastor." Mrs. Ollen sobbed.

Five days later, while every one was sitting around waiting for the funeral band to come and pick the family up, the grand children whispered among themselves about what to do with Madear Ollen as Noah sat silently in the midst of them.

"So, all of us agree that none of us are able to take care of Madear, and she can't stay in this house by herself, we've got to put her in a nursing home." One of the grand children said.

Noah gasped to himself as he lowered his head and whispered a prayer. Mrs. Ollen was in the bed sleeping while her grand children sat deciding what to do with her.

"We've got our on families to take care." Another one whispered almost shamefully.

Noah got up to go into Mrs. Ollen's room to prepare her for the news that he knew she would not want to hear coming form the grand children that she and her husband had on many occasions denied themselves and struggled to raise.

The door creaked open as Noah slowly walked into her room. She lay there peacefully. A thousand thoughts race through his mind of happier times at the church with Mr. and Mrs. Ollen and their five children. He rubbed the gray hair out of her face, and started to speak, but then he noticed that she was not breathing. Quickly he turned to go for help, but suddenly stopped in his steps. He turned back to her bedside, leaned over and kissed her gently on the forehead and whispered softly, "Sleep on old soldier; God has already decided what to do with you."

Dear John

I am suppose to be happy now
I am suppose to be through with you
And over you

But nobody has told my heart
For it refuses to let you of memories of you
And replace you with some other
It clings to wonderful yesterdays
And forgot about the many awful fights
And foul words that were thrown

Oh how my very flesh longs for you
I miss your gentle touch
Your sweet lips
Your warm embrace

They say that I should be happy now
But happy, I am not
For even sleep flees from me
And rest hides its self from my grasp

I am no longer whole
For the other half of me is gone
My bed go lonely
Craving to feel your warm touch just
before the breaking of day

How awful life is
To not realize the worth of a love until it is gone

I miss you
I miss you
I miss you
If I should utter thus thousands of times
Still it wouldn't reflect how deeply I miss you

No one will ever take your place
For my heart refuses to vacate your space
And make room for another

We use to enjoy long walks and soft talks
Now, lawyers tell us what we are to say to each other

I weep bitterly inside
Watching you across the court room

The light in my heart flickers out
At even the thought of someone else taking my place
For your lips were my lips
Your kisses only belonged to me

I often wish that we could go back to yester years
When we were not so driven by money or things
And a big pay check
When friends were diamonds
And family was gold

Now my tears soil my pillow
From thousands of thoughts of you
Hoping that my losing you is but a dream
And I shall awaken soon
From this never ending loneliness

And this sea of advice from those who feel not my pain

I don't want to say it
But I still love you
Oh how much do I still love you

It pains me
At the realization that I must move on
For already you have found a new love
So what we had is now gone
But why do I still weep
When now, with another you share your bed

I wonder do you ever think of me
As I often do you
And wish that we had tried again
To make our relationship work
Before so called friends started advising us

We realized too late
Hurting people desire others to hurt too
As wounded people want to wound others

But I love you still
I miss you still
There is a hole in my heart
That seeps tears for you . . . . for
you . . . . for you . . . . for you

Just Beautiful You

Oh where did you come from, or who did hide you
For there be but none as sociably wonderful as you
Bringing out the best in me as a flower the morning dew

Just beautiful you

My heart, my heart is simply pierced through
With wonderful captivating thoughts of you
And the simple simply wonderful things that you do

Just beautiful you

You slew me with just a kiss
And unveiled my soul what I had miss
Bringing me forth to forever bliss
And tearing down the walls for which I sacredly piss

Just beautiful you

You set me free
And there is where you captured me
I look into your eyes and I see me
There, in the locks of your arms where I am suppose to be

Just beautiful you

You taught me how to love again
And showed me how to live without someone to blame
For my awful hurt and disdain

Just beautiful you

Akeam Simmons

You are my fire and my single flame
That helped me to walk again without shame
No longer a spectator in this love game
But a participant in the love game

Just beautiful you

At the alter you will stand with a ring diamond loaded
Standing there together as our vows are quoted

Bathing in a love that will never be tame
As we share the same last name

Just beautiful you

Proverbs

-Our conversations
Are dominated by the life we live

-If you wish to remain friends
Never seek to promote a friend

-Power unveils the true nature of a man

-Your worst enemy is a woman's scorn
There is no end to her desired occasions to bring much pain

-Be not deceived by a woman's love
For at the very same time
She can hate you just as much
She can kill you and then weep for you at your funeral

-Men are but dogs
So choose the best among them
The worst dogs are the one that lick their own vomit
And the one that chase their own tales

-There is no pain without purpose
There's no service without suffering
There's no sacrifice without reward

-We are born to die
And die to live

-We travel among the dieing
On our way to dwell among the living

-You'll find God on the unbeaten path

-Eternity is but a breath

-The greatest news for a dieing man
Is that God is real

-Taking prisoners during times of war
Exposes you to even more of the enemy's attacks
As holding hostages is a dangerous undertaking

-Let not sleep find your eyes when
your enemy gazes upon you

-You cannot live until you die

-A woman will never love a man that she cannot respect

-Our thoughts and actions
Are the result of what we have gone through
Or yet going through
Thus it is difficult for a wounded man to speak peaceably

-Friendship is stronger than time itself

-Misery is optional
Joy is optional
Thus, I choose where I shall be

-The measure of a man is how he handles his storms

-Forgiveness is something you must receive
And most gladly give

-Life is always made easier by your out look

-If you do not like what you see
Change the way you look at them

-A man is no greater
Than the people he choose as friends

-Religion is but a virus that surrenders everything around
it, but it is a paradox, for men are but brute beasts without
it. They fight and resist all, even themselves, for there is
no loyalty even among their own ranks. They turn on
their own brother as quickly as they would their enemy.

-Ever remind the Negro that he is no longer a slave

-The Negro's worst slave master is himself

-Be careful not to dig your grave with your spoon

-Never cease to live among the stars

-He that retains his youth shall never grow old

-Old age is not a state of the body; it is of the mind

-You've never had a friend-no not one; for
all men seek fortune in some form

-You can never understand a woman, for
she is as complex as the universe

-All men are but brute pirates, for they
ineptly steal, plunder, kill, and destroy.
The best of them is also the worst of them

-Never allow yourself to merely be your lover's option

-You will never rule a mercenary

Lion Wings

Here I walk boldly upon breaths of lion's wings
Into a den among those that wish me no good
Among enemies that use to be friends and lovers

I walk
I stand because there is a greater power
that envelopes me, holds me
And keeps me standing, and fights with me and for me

They seek my life
But they didn't give it to me
So they can't take it from me
They only force me to walk more closely to my God

I grow stronger day by day
My faith is forced to increase
Under which I stand
I breathe the breath of relief
For now I know it is not me
But the power that dwells in me

I am a lion with wings
I fly to yonders mountain
A mountain of peace and tranquility
A mountain of preparation and planning

I fly down to the valleys
Upon enemies whose under estimated me
Who fail to see my sharpened claws
And my ravenous teeth
And my unquenchable appetite for battle

They become bread to quench the beast in me
The beast who is a lion with wings

They be blind
But I see in the darkened night
Traps and snares that they have laid for me

I'll not be fooled by their soothing words
Or their smiling faces
Or their false handshakes

For I am a lion with wings
So my enemies become my prey

Longed Happiness

Oh for from the distant shores
Sails happiness just beyond my reach
I stand upon the shore
Unable to swim that far
So I stand and hope that it shall float unto me

Before I leave these familiar shores

Oh that my heart would cease to cry out
And my soul would scream no more
My breaths be but fumes of passions desire
Filled with hopes and yearnings for a lovers gentle touch

A midnight's winter's heat
Filled with longed passion
Endless passion so deep

I thirst
Undeniable, unquenchable
But still I fight to control my beast

A beast that's sometimes too strong for me
It yields but sleepless nights
And uneasy mornings filled with frustration's delight

But still I stand upon these shores
Catching a glimpse of happiness as it sails
Just beyond my mortal reach

Black Like Me

You are black like me
So you snap when wronged like me
Because we share the same reality
Trying to escape this part given us by society
Blind to us, our condition they refuse to see

Black like me

Color makes you and them insecure
Which give birth to thoughts that's not pure
They won't live in our hood, they'll only tour
So this leaves you feeling unsure
And feeling like less than their pasteurize manure

Black like me

Injustice and racialism have made you want to be white
But it is not so easy to escape this plight
So in the midst of anger, you are forced to fight
And take a stand for what's right
You fight with all your sacred might
To keep some one who looks like you in your sight

Black like me

You bleach your skin and fry your hair
And blue contacts for your eyes you even dare
But still you find it hard to escape this nightmare
Because you are still black like me you are forced to care

Black like me

Because what happens to me happens to you
Even though you have moved into their
neighborhood, injustice still finds you
Talk their talk and walk their walk and hide if you must too
But you can't eternally hide the real you

Blake like me

Wake up before it is too late
And ceiled is your fate
Love yourself and have no one you care enough to hate

Black like me

Black is beautiful
White is beautiful
Red is beautiful
Yellow is beautiful

And when blended together and stretched out across the sky
No one asks why
They're just amazed at how beautiful the
different colors are standing in the sky

Black like me

Be happy with who you are and embrace you
For when you embrace you, you embrace me too
And together we'll embrace the other
colors before the day is done too

Black like me

Made It Through

Out of my storm I have come
Battered, cuts, and bruises, I have some
New relationships I shown
Cause new or regenerated love, I have none
For real feelings I long ago pawn
Like turf pretending to be grass on a fake lawn
I smile to hide my unrelenting pain to some
And to others I am just numb

Now, I am suppose to be happy they tell me
For like a blind man, happiness I fail to see
Cause it alludes and flees from me

My real story has never been told
For it is sometimes too painful to fully unfold
Just know that I have gone through
fire and tried like pure gold
But still I face my storms like a beaten man that's too bold

I stand wanting, for failed relationships
have made me too cold
Hard be it to find a real mate to hold
For often by someone else they have been mold
Like a run away slave that's been too many times sold

Even though many a times I've been broken
And my deliverance has only been a token

Still I shall come through
As I often do
For only I hold the strength to turn my grey skies blue
Until it mend again anew

Still In Love With You

I miss you
Though I try to be strong while I try to get over you
My heart remains blue
Because of my nightly cries over you

Like the morning dew
Precious moments of joy are fleeting too
For my heart still belongs to you
And how to move on, I have not a clue

My emotions multiply and rage like a city zoo
All thrown together and mixed up like grandma's zesty stew
Hot and smothering me like coffee that just left brew

I put on an act in public view
Trying to show that I am over you
But I have become undone inside cause you were my glue
That helped hold it together while I grew
Out of my adolescence that was too awful too

New relations and new lovers I shew
I still want the old, care I not for the new

I walk isolated and lonely for I withdrew
From all those advisers and pity party crew

Now alone talking to God on an empty church pew
And I wonder silently has he dumped me too
I exhale with a relieving whew
And hope that someday I'll get over you too

Can I Touch You Again

I wish that I could touch you just one last time
But hope and pray that somehow I will find
A way to restore this broken heart of mind

I wonder did I do everything I could
As obviously your new lover would
To rebuild and let not dwindle our love that should
For down through the years it stood

I grow weary of people advising me
People who cannot see
What is best for you and me

Inside I scream
Cause during my midnights I dream
Of a broken heart that must be wean
From a love that no longer beam

Desperately I try to hide my brokenness
I try to walk in my best
But truth be told, without you, I feel less
And my emotions are simply a mess

At night my heart chime
Of a richer and happier time
When once we danced and sipped fine wine
With hearts of love so we dine

And as much as I pretend, I still miss you
Still miss your gentle touch, I miss you
My days of sunshine are turned cloudy and blue
For no one ever made me feel as you
You always could make my heart coo

Now you are no longer my lover; you said we were through
Still, I miss you
Miss the you that the world and ungodly friends slew

I must go on, for I have no choice
You broke my heart and silenced my voice

While I can fool others, I fail to fool myself
You will always be a part of me, for in
me, some of you is still left

I miss you
I will always love you
If I could just touch you again as I use to

A Woman's Tears

Like pearls resting upon the bed of the sea
Like diamonds in Africa's budding black hills
Like gallant streams oozing down the mountain side
So precious are her tears

She has wept for kings and peasants
Wept for strangers who were hurting
Wept for kindred who were close but sometimes lost
And even wept for misguided enemies who wished her harm

She weeps for her children who were butchered by life
She weeps for those that are yet in her womb
Yet to be birth so untimely

She weeps for her husband who's denied to be but a man
She weeps for her sons whose dreams
have already been aborted
She weeps for her daughters who's learned to enjoy
And become comfortable being a man

Oh, how her tears flow
Never cease to flow
Her tears are but drops of alluring passion filled
The very heavens notices her tears
Angels carry every one of her drops of water to heaven
And lay them upon the altar of God
God keeps her tears close to his heart

Her tears have saved nations
Conquered kings
And over-thrown enemies

Her tears save the children
And strengthen the men
Her tears help boys become men
and little girls become ladies
Her tears keep husband strong

Her tears is but the glue that holds the whole world together

I am because of her tears
I was because of her tears
I shall be because of her tears

Weep on my dear precious under valued queen
For if your tears ever cease to flow
We shall become but a bubble upon the sea
Who shall burst long before it is time

A woman's tears . . . . Oh how precious

Proverb

-You will have no enemy
Worse than an enemy who use to be your friend

-Bitterness sucks sweetness from the heart

-Never hate your enemy
it confuse your judgment

-Building better relationships make better people

-You cannot give
Without first receiving some of that which you give

A Broken Heart

I long
I hope

I pray for you to awaken out of this horrid nightmare
That has separated us and made us enemies
Wish that I could still hold you in my arms
And wipe away all of your tears
And ease all of your pain
But now another sleeps in my bed
And enjoys the comforts that I once had
I don't want to move on
But it hurts so very badly where I am

I only hope that soon you will see
That I am better than you would allow yourself to see

Oh please awaken out of this stupor
Before we are completely destroyed by our yesterdays
Your new lover can't possibly love you
As much as I do

And even though now you despise me
I still love you

There will always be a place in my heart
That belongs to you
Now I go broken and bleeding
And hurting
And there is no medicine
That can cure a broken heart

Blessed

Bless be the strings that bind
For they bring hope when life is unkind

Bless be the lips that sooth
A broken heart that's blue

Bless be the hands that comfort
And ease a little happiness back in somewhat

Bless be the feet that guild
That help restart a heart that had died

Bless be the heart that remains open
Even after it's been bruised, battered, and broken

Bless be the one that choose to love again
And blossom from which love began

Bless be the foot steps that follow God
For he is the keeper of love's pod

Be A Rock

While doing my morning walk
I wondered upon a little rock
That seemed out of place in its surroundings
I picked it up and wondered
How many times it had been stepped
on or over by so many others
Who had just kept on going
I wondered how many storms that it had gone through
But it still just sat there silently enduring
Whatever came and went

I picked it up
And carried the little rock home with me
And placed it upon my mantle
To remind me to always be a little rock

Sometimes being stepped on
Sometimes being stepped over
Sometimes being thrown away
Sometimes going through
Sometimes folks walking away from you

But knowing full well
That somewhere God will send somebody along
To come and pick you up
And carry you to a place
Where you'll be appreciated for who you are
And what you are

Just a little rock
That refuses to be anything else but a rock

Step on me
But I am still here
Pick me up and throw me away
And I shall still be a rock
Wherever you throw me

When I am having a tough day
I look at the little rock on my mantle
To strengthen myself to keep on going

We need more rocks in our lives
We ourselves need to be a rock
A rock is something that is hard
Something that has weathered the times and changing times
A rock is something that is strong
And have gone through many of storms
Rainy days and even sunny days
And yet it still stands

People can become rocks
But we cannot allow ourselves to become
so big that we cannot be moved
By the pain and hurt of our fellow man
Nor can we allow ourselves
To become so small until we are easily blown away
By situations, conditions, or troubles

We all need to be a rock
And we all need
Some rocks in our lives

Rocks of hope
Rocks of encouragement
Rocks of faith
Rocks of love
Rocks of forgiveness

The prevailing question that you must ask yourself
Is what kind of rock are you

Keep Flying

I went home to visit my mother
While there, I went to the beach
Where I had gone many times when
I was just a boy growing up
I stood on the shore
And watched a flock of sea gulls
Just feet away from me
Suddenly they all started to fly away
But seemed to be caught in a contrary draft of wind
They were only several feet from me
And I watched them flap their wings
Desperately trying to move forward
But to no avail
They just stayed in that one place
All of them were flapping and crying out
But going no where
The wind was simply too strong
After a few moments
They all just landed on the beach in unison
And waited for the hard current to shift
But there was one sea gull that remained in the air
He kept flapping
Kept screaming out
And like the others
He too didn't go anywhere
But he just wouldn't quit
I just kept looking at him

I though to myself
Whey is this dumb bird going to quit like the rest
He just kept on flapping
Kept on screaming

But going nowhere
Even the sea gulls on the ground
Seemed to be looking up at him and thinking like I was
When is that dumb bird going to give up and come down

Just when I had picked up a sea shell to toss at him
To make him come down
The wind shifted
And off he soared like a rocket
He never had to flap his wings for a long time
He just road that current until I could see him no more
Soon, the other sea gulls that were on
the ground took to the air
But still had to fly against contrary winds

I thought to myself
That is just like life is
As we attempt to walk by faith
Contrary winds are always blowing
And it is so much easier to give up
And join the rest of the quitters and
doubters and faithless folks
Who are sitting around waiting passively
for the winds to shift their way
Waiting for someone to give them a hand out
Waiting for somebody else to change things for them

But we must be like that sea gull that had to fly by himself
Because he refused to quit flying and screaming
Flying and screaming

You might have to cry sometimes
But don't you dare land
You might have to scream by yourself
But don't you dare land
Others might look at you and call you
dumb, stupid, and senseless
But don't you dare land

Cause if you keep flying
Keep praying
Keep yelling out for God
He will cause the contrary winds in your life to shift
And you too will be able to ride those
new winds to greater heights
While those quitters and haters and doubter
and complainers, and faithless folks
Are still where they have always been
Complaining about the contrary winds
And still waiting on somebody to help them out

No matter what
You stay the course
Yes sometimes it is difficult
But keep flying because one day
Very soon
Your winds are going to shift
And shoot you forth to make up for all the toiling
That you have had to endure
So keep flying and don't dare land Scream
if you must but keep flying

My Beloveth

Here I sit impatiently waiting upon my beloveth
A place for which I stand set
Waiting tearing risking my heart on merely a bet
Of hopes of forging forth to leave my regret

Ever journeying alone I fret
For having my soul forged into a constant debt

I flinch at unwavering femininity
And hopeless fleeting beauty
Who constantly binge upon me
And force me to places I can't easily see

I am but blinded mercilessly by my own desire
Raging in my bosom the unquenchable passion of fire
Not even a nights lover for my soul to hire
To free me but a night from my emotional muck and mire
Where all are enslaved by a silver tongue liar
Whose only gift is a coffin or bier

In my agony I still wait for her
As a queen at winter time her adorning fur
To blossom our love back to where we once were

I suck the sweetness from her lips and
embrace the softness of her breast
My beloveth brings out of me my best
That I may conquer my life's test
As I wear her love upon my heart like a flowered vest

Loneliness is but a pest
It stills me through with emotional unrest
And turn my days into nights of teary mess
Causing all to flee form me, even rest

My beloveth, my beloveth, tis my quest
I search for her from east to west
And hope of hope that I might find
a heart that I might infest

I will carry my beloveth love in my chest
Where it will inflame me to face life with more than zest
And not settle to be merely a spectator or only a guest

I will shake the earth and grasp the sun
To find my beloveth before I am done
We will walk in splendor and elegance
and have more than just mere fun
Until together our race on earth is fully run
And life on earth has been spun
And we have none
My beloveth, so I search

A Thief Called Old Age

From the day of you birth
Until your last day on earth
He follows you unyielding like a bad curse
And leave you not until you lie in a Hurst

A THIEF CALLED OLD AGE

He will lie with you like a caring nurse
But like a doctor, he'll take all that is in your purse
It matters not your depth of Bible verse
For from the prophet to the priest, he's made all grow worst
Be not dismayed for you're not his first
He started with Adam and Eve after God's prevailing curse

A THIEF CALLED OLD AGE

He will silently steal your youth and your health

Trying desperately to stop him, some
women spend all their wealth
But he keeps taking from you until there is nothing left
He steals right down to your last breath
Causing you to have an untimely death

A THIEF CALLED OLD AGE

You try to fight him with vitamin
And exercise to keep yourself thin
Watching carefully where he has been
But still he steals from you even from within

A THIEF CALLED OLD AGE

He steals your youth and vitality
And a host of things you'd like to be
Wonderful things you cannot see
Like doctor, lawyer, astronaut or some specialty

A THIEF CALLED OLD AGE

He comes and steals even your mother
Breaking and wounding your heart like no other
Yet he sticks with you closer than a brother
And chastens you harder than a father
Forcing you to wonder why ever bother

A THIEF CALLED OLD AGE

You look in the mirror and you see his hand upon your face
All your life he has given chase
But sadly you know you cannot win this race
So during your life make haste
Cause you have no time to waist

A THIEF CALLED OLD AGE

He takes right down to how you even taste
And your steps he forever trace
You pray mightily for God's divine grace
Cause old age you don't won't to embrace

A THIEF CALLED OLD AGE

So now you must make haste
Cause soon in heaven you will plead your case
With old age you'll lose the race
Then some undertaker will put you in a grave or some vase

A THIEF CALLED OLD AGE

Resurrection

I want to truly know God
And the power of his resurrection
I want to embrace his wisdom
Thus setting my imprisoned soul free

I have seen him but I have not looked at him
I have embraced him but I have not felt him
I have drank from his cup but never
tasted the content there in
He has touched me but I have never touched him

Oh wretched man that I am
For I be imprisoned by this ever failing flesh
Enslaved by the ever dieing things around me
Things for which have little value

A rose by any other name is still but a rose
A dog shall never become an eagle
And a hog can never become a gentleman
I be the only crowning creature who is constantly becoming
I am constantly changing, constantly evolving

Though my flesh is dieing
I cannot but live
For something greater lives in me that will never die
Though the sun burns out and the moon ceases its glow
I shall never die

After my flesh has corrupted
And journeyed back to that place from which it was taken
And though my eyes close to never reopen again
And though my breaths be stilled
And though my house become the canker worms meal
I shall still but live
I shall never die
I shall never be destroyed

I shall only be changed and become him
Not like him, but truly him
For I was never severed from him
Life just taught me to be less than who I am
Less than the breath of my Father
Less than the power of his resurrection
But now I have been resurrected even before death
Now, because of my resurrection
No force can stop me
No power can contain me
There is only but me enveloped in the
power of his resurrection

Now I soar like the eagle
And sometimes crawl as the beetle
And cluck undiscernibly as the duck
Because of the power of his resurrection
I become all things to all things
I am but the creature's creature
Who am the epic power of God's resurrection power

Another Day

It be early morning, another day ushers in
Another day to fight the rains of sin
A day I shall fight to conquer and win
And sound the night be gone as a rooster to a hen

I slept far too long
Slept my way right out of my home
No crown now to display, it's too gone
I fight not to be cold down to my bone
And walk in my Fathers forgiveness as I have been shown

It's another day to smile and relish me
And hope upon hope that today I shall be
The man that God chose to set free
To open my eyes for the first time to see

Another day's toils press upon me
Foils that I be not quick to hurriedly flee
For they force me to bow my knee
And change this cup of troubles to that of heaven's tea

Thrust upon me
My Father's key
To change my sadness to unyielding glee
Where God includes me when he said to the heavens We
So there lies my hope of sweet victory
When today I allow God to show his face through me

Halt

I sit on the hymnals of day and night
Hoping for evening and dawn
The ending of my night and the ushering in of a new day
I sit not in either
For I am caught in the twilight of my day
And the very midnights of my nights
But still I sit between the two
For my nights hide my pain and misery
My days dry my tears only leaving stains for my night

I sit hoping for a day of love
A night filled with two lover's passion
Where day and night become one
And time cease to be relevant

A time when my lover will kiss my pain away
And allow me to trust but once again
Kiss Kiss, the kiss of Love
Where all my faults and weakness are covered and yielded

I guard my heart
Never once again to be thrust through by so called friends
Friends who took advantage of my naïve mind
An old goat that pierced an already wounded sheep

I pray to forgive
But forgiveness don't come easily
When every night my lonely bed reminds
me of that stealing devil

My soul ponder how long I had been a fool
And my mind answers far too long

But I cannot entirely blame the devil
For stealing what I thought was mine
Every lover is led astray by their own lust

But I can't reason my pain away
Still I want to castrate that goat
That stole my heart
I am sure just for sport

Secrets

My secrets I must not unveil
Cause my fellow will convict me to hell
And all who will listen he will tell
Of how so very badly I have fell

I must keep to myself
Cause all have been taken I've nothing left
Except hurt, pain, misery and death

But still I have breath
Blessed to be in good health
And the possibility to see another day gives me wealth

I feel sometimes so empty and deaf
I silence my Father's blessings of wealth
And place my faith on misery's shelf
Allowing my mind to suffer great theft

They say um not suppose to cry
But during my nights I weep and
moan and ask my Father why
These tears won't stop coming no matter how hard I try
And sweet sleep I can't even buy

But I force my heart to sing of victory song
And in my nights I bellow that this can't last long
No matter how much hurt I feel, I force myself to be strong

Declare not defeat of me for God is not through with me yet
So against me you shouldn't bet
No matter how many traps have been set

Even though the goats and wolves rage, I will not fret
Put more on me than I can bare, still my Father won't let
To no man is my soul in debt
For my Father won't allow me that regret

Though the pain is severe, I'll come through
Cause I always do
I know that very soon my Father will
make my dark clouds blue

Sipping

I see you over there sitting in the shadow
Sipping on something to make you mellow
Hoping to stop your painful bellow

Trying to forget those that built your gallows
And forced you to live not trusting any fellow
Whose trying to make crooked your halo

You sip and sip and lay low
But lay low too long and they'll think you are yellow
And force you to become some strange fellow

But of that state you must hurry before you wallow
Before the sun rise in your fellow
And the Son take away your halo

So chill like jello
And make your enemies wonder why you're so mellow
It is not in the sip but the fellowship that makes you mellow
Knowing full well that the trap they set
for you ere their own gallow

Now put the sip down
Before the Father frown
And take away your heavenly crown
And you be berried in some forsaken town
Where in misery you will drown
Never to adorn your heavenly gown

Foiled

I walk amidst drops of rain
Trying to hide my tears
Don't want others to know I am human still
Broken, bleeding, wounded I weep
Try to get pass being forsaken by my love
In the morning sunshine I boast of how strong I be
But sometimes the rain come and rescue me
From the lies of strength
I so foolishly try to convey
I am broken
I hurt
Thinking of another kissing lips that were once mine
Over and over
I ask myself
What did I fail to do
Or what wrong things I did
Hopelessly I walk in the rain
Toiling with hurt wrenching thoughts of you
Of how happy we use to be
With very little but love
In our quest to gain much stuff
We lost our love
And opened the door for a fein to come in and steal
I see you and you are over me
But I can't seem to get over you
So in the rain
My heart yearns for you
I blow you a kiss between the rain drops
And hope that it will find you
And tire you of those foreign lips that you now use

Without A Woman's Touch

Above the stars and beyond the moon
Right adjacent to the searing sun's noon

There, oh there lies a woman's touch
Soft and gentle, sexual, filled with such and such
She delivers my soul of a foiling daily crunch

Like an early morning's brunch
Or the flare of a glamorously dressed up Dutch
She lures my soul into her loving clutch
Born with such grace she possess not even a hutch
Of how she soothes with just her touch

I awake to my midnight's sweat
Only to find my earthly flesh most wet
The dark solitude of my bed fills me with regret
Merely a dream of her touch my passion not met

As a poor man amidst a mountain of debt
I weep I morn, I fret
Like a losing gambler's last bet
Hoping against hope that she'll find me yet

I be an hungry hunter casting my net
Fearfully trying to catch a lioness to make my pet
Pierce me through and hollow me as your healing vet
While a table filled with many nights passion I set

The hymn of her dress is as the beautiful endless peaceful shores
Created to complete me, she is the one that I adore
She desires a lion not a sheep, now hear me roar
Hoping to be the king that guards your door

Another Me Too

What great passion of lust
What great piety and virtue
Lies within me

From where it comes, I know not
where it goes I do not know
Oh wretched man that I am

Caught between the two
For I love piety and virtue
But I too love the passion of lust just as much

How can this be
There are two of me coexisting as one
Piety and wickedness abiding in the same house

Like east and west, north and south
Opposites, but existing upon the same axis

It seems that one defines the other
One has no meaning without its opposite
Good is cherished because there is bad
And evil is magnified because there is good

There exist a level between the piety and the lust
That produces me
As a drunken man, I stagger in steps I cannot long maintain
My head spins and I ma fearful
For I know not when the other me will surface
And defuse the other me

Or which is the rel me
My thoughts betray me
For when I try to live virtuously
My mind screams dark thoughts of pleasure to be

Lust be wanting everything
And never having enough

Virtue is declare enough when there is not enough
To win, I must subdue the lust and proclaim
the virtue, for therein is strength

Nit Wit

Because I am a little slow mentally
People treat me strangely
Even my friends and family

When I come into the room they whisper about me
And shawn me even though we are family
Don't they know that even a nit wit can be
Emotionally hurt too, even when he is slow to see

So I act like I don't understand, but I do
Nit wits have feeling too
I just walk around while my anger brew
Just an over looked nit wit that they never really knew

While I am slow to understand the whys and the wherefores
And me, a pretty lady will never adore
I do know when a person is treated less than a whore
Like something so vile, they have never seen before

Sometimes I feel I can take no more
Being treated like a dog on the floor

I think it is better being a nit wit and have a heart
Than be sane with emotions that have fallen apart

So when I am talked to I act like I am slow and don't hear
Then they are careful because they fear
Of what might come of me being so near

Than be like them, I would rather remain a nit wit
Rather than be heartless like them and fit

Through Injustice

Being judged because of he color of my
skin brings me much irritation
And they wonder why I am sometimes
aggressive and display aggravation
Being force to see these hope for my annihilation
I am catapulted into thoughts of violent agitation

No need to ponder or pierce deep meditation
Or even journey to the farthest realms of your imagination
Daily I am pierced through with horrid deprivation
And a constant torrent of degradation

They build bigger and more prisons for my incarceration
Hoping to kill the king in me into hopeless limitation
And severe my dreams, my nerves, and even my imagination
Desiring to cease and bury all of my motivation
To change my situation and place me
into mental incarceration

Secretly and openly I am constantly under investigation
They steer me down crooked paths
that produce no deviation
But like a pastor to his congregation
I seek to look past them and bring them and
myself to higher spiritual levitation

So I endure the negative allegation
Which sometimes force me into civil costly litigation
Or some empty bias mediation

In the belly of the beast, I pray for revelation
And even among my adversaries and I seek out information

That will inevitably give me mental exaltation
To change this marred hopeless indignation
Cast upon me from the first steps of
my unholy forced migration
From Africa to a host of places of molestation

There sit old wounds upon me filled with inflammation
For still I am forced into civil isolation
Secretly governed and profiled by unjust regulation
For which they thrust their own connotation

I am forced to rise to new higher spiritual inspiration
Every time I am knocked down I get back
up with new determined revelation
Of how to change my own situation
Positive thinkers who believe in themselves
shall by my constant congregation
Until I break these emotional and
psychological pains given justification
I'll not sit around and hope and wait
for some new legislation
To bring about my civil salvation
No, I'll carry my hopes and dreams upon
my back like new crustation
Ever marching forth to my freedom with no reservation

Even the thought of justice and freedom
elates me with thrilling sensation
Pushing aside all of my frustration

The King in me press forward with no hesitation
To be treated justly like a man is my destination

Scars

I look on my body and I see the things I've gone through
And a host of bad situations I longed slew
Some deep, some long, some fresh too
Reminding me of my suffering as the Jew

Most of my scars are longed cure
But the emotional pain lingers that's for sure
In my nakedness my scars present me insecure
As others look and wonder how I endure

Though most of them were easy to heal
The emotional pain I carry still
And sometimes I am eased with a pill
Still my body and mind refuse to congeal

The perpetrators are long gone and afar
But still each one of them left an everlasting scar
And try as I might to forget sipping in some lonely bar
Still the scars protrude from me like breast in a braw

Wish that I could hide my scars tucked away in some jar
And ride around town carefree in my car
Shining and beaming and glowing like a distant star

My scars let me know that what I went through was real
Of the many horrific things I had to deal
Some though cured I am still not completely heal
So on my knees I constantly kneel
Praying to God for his perfect will
And the strength to continue to move on still
Until all the pain from me is peal

Raindrops

Thank God again outside it rain
Washing away yesterday's pain
And situations that nearly drove me insane
But still I remain

Wonderful purely raindrops
That water our crops
And rinse our mops

Through the raindrops I leap and hop
Feeling like it rinses me from all of my flops
Filling me with such joy that I feel I would pop
And again shoot forth back on top

Oh let it rain
Let it rain
When all of my pain is washed away I'll have none to blame
If I but continue to walk among shame

Please raindrops bath me through
That I'll be over the hurt that I've gone through
And ready myself to love and live life anew

Proverbs

-If you're not getting resistance
You're probably not pushing forward

-The worst prisons are the ones with
no bars, or locks, or cells

-All men are but hypocrites pretending
to be something they're not

-Words spoken during anger are bitter truths

-always give your adversary space to retreat
Else you force kill or be killed

-Luck will always seek out practice and preparedness

-Dignity leaves us with excuse

-Men can only hurt you inside when you allow them inside
They can only make you feel what you already feel

-No water can be drawn from a dry well

-Oh what miserable lives we lead
When we live lives to deceive

-You will never die until you stop living
One always choose their time to die

In-sane

Desperately I try to control
My mind, my body, and my soul
Of lessons that's always been told
Of men that are too callously bold
Whose hearts are hardened and cold

Where do I parlay
And infiltrate the winding night of day
To drive the dispelling darkness of despair away
So our teachers can have something weightier to say
To our children who just want to play

The world is a melting pot of crazy
I find it most difficult to keep my sanity
Because I don't want to be like
everybody, I just want to be me
And create my own world of relative reality
Where I can live in the subconscious mind of immortality

Osama Ben Laden, Sadam Husane
Are just two more too crazy men to blame
For our unresolved evoked shame
Of unequivocal selfness that shoot
forth man's arrows of disdain

I must find holy resolute courage
And put my fear and hurt in psychological voyage
Through pain and despair that's almost too painful to tour it

Secretly I wonder who's really insane
Is it the refusal to conform and be tame
Or the ones that's willfully homeless
and is content with no gain
No, it be those that have allowed their
minds to become impotently lame

The Game

You say you don't want a player
But why do you try to play me
You force me to be who you say you
Say you don't want me to be
I am only playing the game
You made the rules

You will never stop the game
But you can change the rules
The game is in me
The rules are in you
You taught me

Demand more
And I will give you more
Expect nothing
And I will give you less

I only follow your rules
I am simple
Only the basics of instincts govern me
My flesh, my flesh slays me

Oh please save me
No matter how I act
I am only following your rules

I will climb as high as you want me to
Or climb not at all if you should keep silent
When you look at me
You see a reflection of you

I am what you created me to be
So if you want me to change
You must first change
Because I only follow the rules
Your rules

Exhale

We be shallow and fake
Living lies we refuse to forsake
How much misery can we take
Before we decide to awake
And be free from a life we simply hate

For here I am self to be
Hidden deep inside of me
A me that others never do see
Cause they don't want to know the real me
Only the me I pretend to be

Have I already died and gone to hell
Living a life that is a hollow shell
With no love and no joy to even tell

How I lost or fail
Hoping to exit this chose prison without bail
So here I stay in my invisible cell
Waiting to some day to simply exhale

Change

You are what you were
And you will always be
What you have always been

To look at your ancestors
Is to look into life's mirror
To change who I will become
I must change who I am right now
Change is difficult and painful
But I realize that there is significant purpose to my pain

Change will not become complete without pain
Pain like fear is a gift to me
A warning system to alert and alarm

For needed positive change
I must never allow myself to become dull
And numb to my pain and fear

For in so doing I limit myself to rise
No higher than my ancestors
And close the doors to any positive
Change to me and my offspring

Caught Up

Sarah sat on the front pew as she watched her mother, Dr. Gail Latil, sooth her anxious listeners. Mrs. Latil was not a preacher or evangelist; she was a heart specialist in the local hospital. She was lecturing at the church on caring for your heart. Sarah was amazed at how good her mother was at lecturing and how much passion she produced for her topic, and how much compassion she seemed to have for her listeners. She fiddled thoughtlessly with a bible. How can she be so successful in public, and such a failure in private, thought Sarah. Father is such a sweet gentle, and caring man, but he is too passive-down right Hen peck; she thought wearily. In public, mother spoke to him kindly and gently as a wife should speak to her husband; but in private, she is harsh and cruel to father. She speaks to him any kind of way with little or no respect. He just takes it; Sarah thought angrily.

What Sarah didn't know was that Mrs. Latil was ashamed and embarrassed of where Donald, Mr. Latil worked. He was a supervisor at the town's waist control plant. She thought that he was beneath her. She only stayed with him because her church frowned on divorce, and all of her associates seemed happily married. But, Gail was miserable; it was a private hell. She sought refuge at the hospital in the friendship of a heart surgeon-Dr. Maxwell. She was completely happy with her long time friend Dr. Maxwell. Gail would work late just to be able to spend a little more time with him. They took breaks together, and afterwards, retired to the doctor's lounge and talked for hours at a time. Gail and Maxwell would often meet at medical conventions; some days, they would not attend the meetings, and just go out and tour the city until late in the night.

Gail was desperate to get out of her miserable marriage without losing any of her coveted social respect. She sat and stared in the mirror at how beautiful she was as she thoughtlessly brushed her long hair. She peered over her shoulder and sneered at the disgusting snoring man in her bed. Such an uncultured thing; he doesn't deserve me; she thought to her self.

Sarah stared aimlessly at the television; she was furious-angry at her mama for being so mean and cold to her daddy, and angry at her daddy for being so passive, and angry at God for putting her in such a house. She noticed her mother out the corner of her eyes exiting the door. Her father sat at the kitchen table, face still red and bruised where Gail had slapped him with a brush, sipping on a cup of coffee. Just before shutting the door behind her, Gail rang out, Have a good day sweetie."

Sarah didn't reply.

"Sarah." Gail said more sternly.

"Okay mother, I will."
She took a few steps down the stairs and hollered back, "This yard looks atrocious; it better be done when I get back."

"Yes dear, I will get it done." Donald yelled back without changing any expression; he just continued sipping his coffee. Sarah and Donald could hear Gail mumbling as she entered the car.

"Good for nothing son of Satan, ain't no man." Gail said to herself.

As she drove to the office, she thought of how wonderful it would be if Maxwell was her husband and Sarah's father. That's when Gail began the sick twisted plot to get rid of her husband of 15 years.

A Year had passed and Gail and Dr. Maxwell were simply in love. She had to some how get rid of Donald without the stain of divorce. At work, for months she had lied and cried on anybody's shoulder that would listen to her of how badly Donald treated her and how he constantly threaten to leave her without a trace. After a while, her plan started working; all of her associates thought that Donald was a complete brute that didn't deserve Gail. They often asked her, "Has he left yet?" and, acting sadly, Gail would reply, "Not yet.".

Six months had passed; her plan was ready. She came back home from the hospital early; had allowed Sarah to sleep over at a friend's house. She prepared a wonderful dinner that evening. Donald was overcome with joy; silently he thanked God for changing his wife. They took a slow bubble bath together. Afterwards, she rubbed and messaged him down with warm fragranced oil. They went to the kitchen o a candle lit prepared dinner. She had cooked all of his favorites. Donald just kept saying, "I love you Gail."

She kept saying, "I know."

Gail looked simply beautiful; her night gown just laid on her. After dinner, she whispered to him, "How about a nice glass of wine before we adjourn into the bed room for deserts." Donald just nodded like a your school boy. She went into the kitchen and swiftly returned with two glasses of red wine. She held her glass up for a toast, "Here's to new wonderful beginnings." He touched her glass, and then gulped the wine down swiftly. She took a sip and sat her glass down. Donald started to get up, but suddenly fell back down grabbing his throat gasping for air. He began to foam from the mouth; his eyes bulged out; his hands balled up; his body trembled.

Swiftly, Gail ran into the bed room and slipped on her dress. She rushed back into the dinning room. Donald was still, eyes bulging out staring aimlessly. Quickly she blew out the candles, and started hurriedly cleaning the table. She lift Donald's head off the plate to lean him back. His body fell lifelessly to the floor.

While the body just lay there, she cleaned he house-getting rid of any evidence of a romantic evening. She bent over and grabbed Donald under the arms to drag him out back. "My God you're heavy." She complained. She realized that there was no way that she could drag Donald across the yard to a grave that he had dug the day before. She told him to dig a deep hole for some house garbage that she didn't want the garbage men to see-he had dug his own grave.

She swirled franticly; her head spinning with a thousand thoughts. With all of her strength, she dragged the body into the garage and managed to get it in the car. She drove to the butcher store. Mr. Galvanolti, the owner, was locking the front doors. Gail knew that Mr. Galvanolti had a tremendous crush on her. She got out of the car and walked gracefully towards him. He smiled broadly like a school boy.

"Miss Gail what brings you out this late?" He said to her with a grin.

"I need your help, and I'll do anything to get it."

"He grinned like child on Christmas morning. "What do you need?" Slowly she stroked her hand through her long silky hear and measured his every gaze. Casually they walked over th to car; she opened the door and the light beamed upon Donald's dead corpse. Galvanolti's cigar fell from his lips. "He's dead. What happened?"

"Never mind what happened. They say that you can make a body disappear without a trace . . . . Well, can you?" She asked nervously.

"Yes . . . . Yes . . . . Yes I can." Stammered Mr. Galvanolti. "But it will cost you Miss Gail."

"Anything." Gail said confidently as she tilted her head back, raised her brow, and ran one hand slowly through her long black hair while the other rested on her sculptured hip.

"Let's go into my office for a minute. Mr. Donald is not going anywhere."

Without turning on any lights in the shop, Mr. Galvanolti led Gail to his office, turned on the light and shut the door behind them.

Forty five minutes later, Gail exited the office, stopped just outside, took a deep sigh, tried to primp her disarrayed hair, straightened her dress, and then gracefully walked through the darken shop back to her car where the dead body of her husband waited. She slid into the car and glanced back at him. "Just like you; never complain no matter what I do." She snapped angrily at the corpse as though he could hear her. "Wish that old fool would hurry up." Finally, Mr. Galvanolti came out of the shop, with his shirt open, wiping sweat from his face. He walked a few feet over and opened a large garage like door, and then walked to Gail's car. "Get out Miss Gail, and wait in the office. This won't be but a minute."

Gail waited in the office; she heard loud machinery running. After twenty minutes, Mr. Galvanolti came back into the office, smiled broadly at Gail and said, "It is done; now let's discuss our new relationship; shall we." He began taking off his shirt.

"Could we have a drink first?" Gail said barely above a whisper now realizing fully what she had gotten herself into.

He reached into his desk drawer, pulled out a bottle of Scotch, and turned to his book shelf and grabbed two glasses. He poured quickly and nervously; spilling Scotch upon the desk as he poured.

"May I have some ice please?" Gail whispered, trying to cause Mr. Galvanolti to leave the room. As he left, swiftly she reached into her purse, grabbed a small bottle, and then poured something into Mr. Galvanolti's glass, stirred it with her finger then sat back down.

He returned with the ice, and dropped two ice cubes in Gail's glass. He reached and grabbed his glass, held it up to toast. "Here's to our new hot relationship."

Gail smiled and touched his glass with her own. He tilted his head back and gulped his drink down. Gail gracefully sipped hers. Mr. Galvanolti grabbed Gail around her waist and pulled her closed to him, and started to kiss her on her neck. Suddenly a burst of pain rushed through his chest, while his throat gasped for air; his fingers crooked up as he dropped to the floor foaming from the mouth.

Gail stood up, rubbed one hand slowly through her long black silky hair, and rested the other on her marvelously sculptured hip, and said, "Men, they are all alike. The things a girl has to do to survive." She said calmly, then looked down at the now still body of Mr. Galvanolti. "Did you really thin that I would leave a garbage man for a butcher-Please."

She raced back home trying to get there to get rid of any evidence of a crime that she might have over looked. Suddenly she saw blue police lights flashing in her rearview mirror. She knew that she could not afford to get a ticket on this side of town; it would be evidence that she was in the vicinity of Mr. Galvanolti's murder. A thousand questions invaded her mind as the policeman walked up to her car.

"Miss Gail, where are you going so fast tonight?" The Policeman said as he looked down on Gail while fumbling with his ticket book. Gail just burst into tears, and explained about her unhappy life and unhappy marriage. "I just need to talk to somebody-be with somebody for a while." She said amidst sobs.

"Well, there is a small diner not far from here, and I am about to take my break; we can talk if you like," said the Policeman.

"Can we go to some place more private? Do you live for from here?" She knew that he was single, for she had met him around town and had caught him gazing at her sculptured body as she walked by him; so, she knew that he already had a crush on her-and tonight, she would play it for all that it was worth.

"Just follow me; I don't live for from here." He turned off his flashing lights and led Gail to his house.

As they sat on the couch, Gail wept and talked. She laid her head upon his shoulder. "Do you have anything to drink?" She whispered as she gazed in is eyes with lips barely inches from his. She pressed her lips against his and gave him a deep long slow kiss, then pull away very slowly.

"Now can I have that drink?"

"Sure . . . . Sure . . . . I'll git it for you."

"And I don't like drinking alone." She yelled after him.

"But I am on duty." He said.

"One little drink with your new secret girlfriend before we make it official won't hurt will it."

"No . . . . No . . . . I guess not."

He rushed into the kitchen and moments later returned with two glazes of Hennessey

"Hennessey?" Gail said surprised.

"What did you think black men drink? We sure don't drink Scotch." He said as he moved closer to Gail and started to kiss her.

"Would you go get me a towel? I've got a treat for you." She said as she pulled away.

Quickly he rushed off into the next room. Gail reached into her purse, grabbed a bottle, and poured into her new found friend's glass and stirred it with her finger. He returned with the towel. She picked up her glass and held it out towards him, "Here's to a night you'll never soon forget." She sipped ; he gulped. Before he could hardly lower his glass, he grabbed his throat and gasped for air as he fail to the floor.

"I won't find out tonight whether it is true what they say about black men." Gail said smoothly as she stepped over him and headed out the door.

Finally, she got back home; exhausted, she needed a drink. Her drink that she had poured with her husband Donald was still on the table. She picked it up, flung her jacket onto the couch and took a big gulp as she walked into the kitchen. She gasped, noticing the glass on the sink with her red lip stick around the rim. She realized in horror that she had mistakenly poured her drink out and left Donald's poison filled drink on the table. A thousand thoughts raced through her mind as she began to gasp for air. Her chest tightened and excruciating pain raged in her stomach. She stammered to the phone, but dropped it because her fingers started to crook and ball up with cramps. Gail fail to the floor, foaming from the mouth, and slipped violently into the clutches of death.

My Angel

I have rode the wings of my dreams waiting for you
Searching for you
As prince charming often do
Hoping that you push back these skies
that's been too long blue

My breaths are short with unyielding anticipation
Shooting forth sweet unbridled imagination
Wonder filled thoughts of love with no reservation

Your radiant beauty puts Cleopatra to strife
And your smile gives even dying roses new life
You are the sweet fragrance a man smells
when he thinks of a new wife

You are a rose amidst a valley of lilies;
your beauty is unmistakable
Your smile is undeniable
And the depth of your warm eyes is unquenchable

You are the end result when God thought
of something wonderful and sweet
And he let down his hand and allowed me one
of his beautiful earthly angels to meet
That forces my heart to have rhythm while it beats

Every man should meet at least one angel during his life
Then the world wouldn't be filled with so much strife

Mama's Love

Mama sat there ashamed as she rubbed medicated ointment on my bruises and open whelps of cuts. I lay there in her lap softly shaking as the stinging pain riddled up and down my body. I could not sit down, for my backside couldn't bear it. Tears rolled down my face as I lay there amidst more emotional pain than physical pain.

I heard her continue to try to utter something sweet to me as she tried to sooth my wounds and calm me down; but it was no use, her words to me were indiscernible; they were drowned out by memories of horrid screams at me, and shouts of how no good I was, and the sound of the continued lashes of the ironing cord as it ripped by flesh with every stroke.

I hurt more inside than I did outside. My own mama beat the hell out of me, like she hated me, and then tried to put medicated ointment on the scars. I believe the ointment was not to ease my pain, but rather to try and hide them from neighbors and the searching eyes of my school teachers.

How could a loving mother force her own daughter to sit in a tub of water just prior to a beating with an ironing cord? Her thought was to whip me right after I got out of the tub, while my body was still wet. She thought that would cause more pain. I think she enjoyed whipping me-she looked forward to it. Sometimes, when she couldn't wait to get me home from school, she would beat me over the head in the car with her shoe while she drove, or stopped at any red light.

One of my high school acquaintances raped me after a ball game, but I didn't tell my Mama because I knew that somehow it would have been my fault and warranted me of another brutal beating. On wash day, when she asked me why was my panties spotted with blood, I didn't tell her because I had been raped; I just said that I didn't know.

I hated when my father left home for work or any reason, for my beatings were always worse when he wasn't there, and she always found a reason to whip me when father was gone; a dirty glass left in the sink, or I didn't wash dishes right, or my room wasn't clean enough, or I left a spot in the bath tub; it was always something to warrant her getting her kicks from beating the hell out of me.

Now, she asks why I don't come to visit her when I only live a short distance away, or why I won't let my son stay too long with her. Her violent outbursts at my father lets me know that the mean witch of a woman still resides in her, and she is just waiting for an opportunity to beat the hell out of my son. No, she'll not lay him across her lap with cuts and whelps covering his body from her brutal beating while she puts medicated ointment on them. No, I'll save my son from my Mama's love.

Now, when I go home, my heart breaks and tears swell in my eyes as I look at my aging father with sometimes fresh cuts upon his arms, or hands, or a bruise upon his head. He just tells me that he fell or something, and then tries to assure me that he is alright, but I knew that he wasn't alright, and he didn't just fall or bump into something . . . . I knew that it was Mama's love.

I hate when my phone rang late at night or in the early hours of morning. I always think that it is the morning that my Mama's love have finally taken away my father.

Bridled Self

I spoke to myself today
Of myself yesterday
About myself and tomorrow

My heart still strolls down the vibrant
isles of my High School
My breaths still breathe my youth
My todays are filled with the sweet melodies of yesterday

My taste buds
Simply refuse to yield to the sweetness
of the wine from new grapes
For it forces all to be but new bitter
nectar poured upon my lips

My heart has hid itself deep within the rocks of my soul
That even I cannot find it
And there resides in me a empty hole
where my heart use to be

Memories of yesterday tortures me
I am agonized by chosen loneliness today
And I am scared of even the thought
of being alone tomorrow

My dreams are still flooded with thoughts of yesterday
Oh that I might wakeup to my loves warmth beside me
And cherish the sweetness of a morning's kiss

But still I go lonely
Walking with myself
Talking to myself
About myself

I am incomplete
For half of me has fled
The whole of me refuse to come together again
And I know not how to control my flesh
That I might move on
But I don't even know if I truly want to move on
For my heart refuse to say
Or has it screamed at me but I am not listening
Oh wretch that I am that my own self has bridled my self

Trash

I am but a piece of trash
That somebody cast beside the road
And nobody wants

I am invisible to all that look my way
The few that see me
Frown upon me for staying beside the road
Where somebody threw me

Soon the great steal monster
Will come and eat me
And carry me where other trash be
Heaps of trash that have been tossed aside
and thrown away just like me

I sit and wait and hope
That somebody will come and recycle me

Life's A Game

The other night I went to a basket ball game to support my youth, which I call all of them my children. I sat and quietly observed three intense games; five players on the court against five opposing players. They ran up and down the court, sweating, tired, straining, trying their very best to get their team ahead. Some took some hard hits, but got right back up and ran to their position-though obviously in pain. It appeared that every one of them was connected to each other; when pressure impacted one player, he simply passed the ball to his fellow team mate that had less pressure. And, I noticed that all of them, both our team and the opposing team, kept an attentive ear to the man on the side lines with the clipboard in his hand-the coach. The coach would call one player to come out, and he would quickly run off the court, while another took his place. I am certain that some of them disagreed with the coach, but none of them showed their disapproval of the coaches decision . . . . For they knew, to stay in the game, and to win, they had to follow their coaches instructions-good, bad, or indifferent. There were parents and spectators in the bleachers-who I call bleacher coaches. They were shouting at the coaches; shouting at the referees, and even at the opposing teams-showing their love and support for their team. I noticed that they would always try to get the players on the court attention-to tell them how to do something, but the players would always ignore them, and stick to their coach's plan-at the frustration of the bleacher coaches.

I thought to myself that life is the same way. God is our coach, and life it self is our referees. There are so many bleacher coaches in our lives that's always trying to show us, or tell us how to do something better or different from what our coach has said. And, just like the young players on the basket ball court, we too will get hit sometimes, perhaps even unfairly, but we cannot lay there and wallow because we've been hurt by someone; we must get back up and take our position. And, sometimes when the pressures of life becomes too much for you to handled, just as the basket ball players passed the ball, you've got to pass it on and allow someone to help relieve you. We've got to ignore those bleacher coaches, for they have not looked at God's clipboard to know his perfect plan for you. Sometimes when you are sweating, and have become too tire, God will pull you out and allow you to rest awhile, but until the coach says that is enough, then keep sweating, keep running, take your hits and get back up . . . . Because just like our basket ball team did, at the end of the night, you'll go home a winner!!!

Yes, I was concern about my sons getting hit too hard, and getting unfair calls by the referees, or being pulled out when I though that they were hot; and yes, I was more than a little concern when I saw my daughter, as a cheer leader, being hoisted high into the air-held up only by a few weak teenager, but I sat back and watched them win respectively . . . . So, I quietly eased out of the gymnasium as quietly as I had came-hoping that sometimes during their game they had seen their spiritual father sitting in the stands quietly supporting them.

Unwanted Cargo

A few weeks ago, I went swimming in the ocean. I dove in the water with my swimming trunks on. I enjoyed the cool refreshing salted water as it splashed upon my body. I swam under water and tried to chase some of the little colored fishes while I picked up a few sea shells on the bottom. When I got out, I thought that I had come out the way that I had gone in-only wet and a little salty; but to my surprise, my swimming trunk's pockets were filled with sand. I didn't purposely try to get sand in my pockets. It just gathered there because of my environment. I thought to myself that life is sometimes the same way. We often times are around people and places, and situations, and conditions, and circumstances that are affecting us and we don't even know it. Before I could go back into my hotel and enjoy the amenities of the hotel, I had to dump the sand out of my pockets and wash it off of my body. It is the same with us in our lives. Before we can move on to greater blessings and expand our boarders, we've got to first empty our emotional pockets. If not, you'll make your new people pay for the way the old people treated you, or you'll carry your old broken issues into your new relationship. STOP!! Empty your pockets, and tell God to wash you off so that you can fully enjoy where he is taking you! Look what God says to us in Jeremiah 29:11: I know the plans I have for you, declares the Lord. Plans to prosper you and give you hope and a future.

My Princess

Oh . . . . Oh . . . fairest maiden of them all
My heart but beats and bleeds of you
I cannot contain no longer; I must come to you

I be but a hopeless bundle of consuming love
Burning . . . . Burning . . . . Burning
So bright that I fill the night
With glimmering bathing light

If there be a mountain
I shall climb it
If there be a sea
I shall swim it
If there be a path
I shall walk it

Whatever the task to become one with you
I be willing and but ready
I conquer the unconquerable for the princess heart

Bow me down so sweet
And feel my heart pound the rhythm of love so dear
Pierce me through with a wonderful you
Oh you . . . . Oh you . . . . You princess
that conquers my heart

My princess . . . . My princess . . . . My princess

Proverbs

-To be of sound mind is the richness of God
To have peace is the blessing of God
To have good health is the mercy of God
To have love is the goodness of God

-Only sacrifice produce greatness

-anxiety is but fear equipping its self
For future times of digest

-Never give another enough power over
you to interrupt your day of delight
For they shall never stop with just interrupting delight.

-Do not delight at the troubles of others
For they are but steps from your front door

-Be gracious, and grace shall follow you home
For the universe demands that you reap
that which you have sown

-Be not despaired at love
For love will find a way

-At the day of troubles
Just hold on, for it shall soon pass

-Every wind that comes
Shall soon pass

-The fool first fools himself
Then seek others to fool

The Caged Bird

I have wings but cannot fly

They sit me in my cage upon their porch
And allow me to see my brother's freedom
My brothers peer at me from branches near by
Scared to come too close for fear of my fate

They think that I sing because I am happy
But I sing to let my brothers know that I am here
And to remind myself that I still matter

I be just something for their luxury
Never thinking of how cruel they are to me

Would that I could be like my brothers
And fly from tree to tree
And awaken every morning searching for something to eat
While cautious of the Hawks in the sky
Wanting to make a meal of me

Unlike my brothers that are free
I eat when I want
I drink a little water when I want
And they cover me up at night to keep me warm
And no cat can pierce my cage to eat me

But still
I want to be free
And fear daily what will happen to me
And search for my daily bread
And climb in a nestle of leaves upon the trees
To keep me warm at night when I sleep

Then I would sing because I am happy
I would sing amongst my brother's songs
And be free to be the bird I was designed to be
And sing, and sing, and sing, and sing

Then I'd get me a man and put him in a cage
And feed him, and show him off to my brothers
And see how he would feel to be caged
For others to see . . . . But, then I couldn't be so cruel

Akeam Simmons

Proverbs

-Be careful in disturbing the giant
For there are great consequences
If he sleeps, let him sleep on

-Never allow your pass to become your present
There is a reason why it is called the pass

-Trust is a very expensive commodity
For which many have purchased in vain

-A people's culture
Is birth from their needs

-You can never raise your children twice

-Ain;t nobody like mama; God only gave you one

I Pray For You

Look at you standing there talking about
how much you love the bible
Reading passed every things that's viable
Hoping to make everyone else liable
Misquoting the convicting things you find undeniable

Call your self a leader but have no vision passed your nose
But you love to teach your personal prose
Jabbering out everything like a woman's running hose
Completely forgetting why he arose
And the sin door he closed

Hoping to find somebody you can teach
And push away from what the pastor preach
Another innocent soul you hope to reach
Before good preaching makes him bleach
From teaching that produces breech
Of God's Word that's so sweet

You stay and bring trouble to the flock
Separating them from the pastor with your unholy block
But the rifle of time has been cocked
To dissemble the false teaching you have docked

Oh but I must pray for you
For the unholy things that you do
Chasing away members from the church that's still new
And the ones that remain you tried spiritually to slew
With that sharp tongue you toss about over every pew

But still I pray for you
Cause hell is filled with people like you
Teaching things that be not true
Forming your own doctrine anew

Still I must pray for you
Cause hell is too horrid a place even for people like you
So I hope that you will change before your sun sets too
Like so many other self righteous people sun's have too

Only prayer can change you
And the awful things that you do
Spreading discord across the pew
Trying to get others to follow you

Still I pray for you
As Jesus would do for people like you

Take Your Seat

The other day, I was at a funeral. I arrived late, and the church was packed. I stood at the back of the church with several other members and a few other pastors. While I stood there paying my respect, one of the ushers walked up to me and said that a man, a few pews over, recognized me, and told the usher to tell me to come and he would give up his seat so that I could sit down. I told him thanks so much, but no thanks; I didn't want to cause a commotion.

Later when I got home, I thought of the incident, and thought of how much that situation paralleled to God's grace through Jesus Christ.

You see, Jesus saw us in a bad fix, so he gave up his seat in heaven to come down so that we would have a seat in God's kingdom; but, many times, we respond to Him just like I responded to the man that offered me a seat . . . . Thanks, but no thanks.

We continue, by choice, to endure what we have been going through, and never yield to God. But, if we would just yield, He will make room for us; and help carry our heavy burdens that life has tossed upon us, or those for which we have chosen ourselves.

He says, "Come and sit at my table while I wipe away all tears from your eyes, and make your enemies your foot stool."

So, be not apprehensive; go on and take your seat for which Jesus has prepared for you . . . . Even when somebody else thinks that it is unfair . . . . But then, favor is not fair, or else it wouldn't be favor!!!

My Best Friend Jesus

One day, while at home relaxing, I got a call from my daughter; she told me that she and her best friend had had a tire blow out on the interstate. I immediately told her that I was on my way. When I got there, they were surrounded by, what seemed like a sea of cars, passing by them with two policemen directing traffic.

When I arrived, they were sitting in the car, seemingly half afraid. Her friend was trying her best to be cool, but I could tell that she was slightly frantic while trying to call for Triple A, or someone, or anyone.

I stepped up and tried to calm them, and show them that they need not worry because Daddy had arrived. We called a wrecker; my daughter said, "But we don't have any money." I told her don't worry about it because "I got this". I paid for the wrecker to pull the car and to change the tire. When he changed the tire, he put on a Donut tire-which wasn't much good; so I told my daughter's friend to follow me to a tire store so that I could have a new tire put on her car-she did.

After having taken care of them, and getting them back on the road to go back to campus, my daughter's best friend told me that her parents would pay me later; I told her don't worry about it; you don't owe me anything.

You see, because she is my daughter's best friend, she naturally becomes one of my daughters as well. I came to her rescue because she was a friend of my daughter; I paid the wrecker because she was a friend of my daughter; I bought another tire for her car because she was a friend of my daughter; I told her that her bill was paid in full and that she owed me nothing because she was a friend of my daughter.

Later, when I got home, it dawned on me that that is how God looks at us during our times of trials and troubles, and emergencies. Because his son Jesus is a friend of ours, we become one of God's children. He heals us when we're sick because his son is a friend of ours; he comes to our rescue because his son is a friend of ours; he gives us grace because his son is a friend of ours, and our sin debt has been paid in full; we owe nothing . . . . Simply because we befriended his Son.

Jesus told his disciples that he no longer called them servants, but friends.

Now, my daughter's best friend has my number, and knows that if she has an emergency, she can always call her best friend's father, and I would come swiftly . . . . Because she is my daughter's friend!!!!!

Make Jesus your friend, and watch the wonderful treatment and favor that God the Father will display towards you because his Son, Jesus, is your best friend.

I Am Still Human

Sometimes our minds are so deeply on heaven until we become no earthly good. Heaven is for those that have transcended flesh and are spirit. We, on earth, are flesh and spirit. Our flesh forces us to operate within the "fleshly" ramifications-thus, we are human, and because we are human, we circum to humanly things. Because we are still human, we mess up sometimes; because we are still human, we make mistakes sometimes; because we are still human, we are prone to inadequacies. It does not mean that we are less holy; it just means that we are holy and human.

So many times, we place extra burdens on ourselves by trying to be "super" human, so when we falter, it is hard for us to even forgive ourselves.

As a Christian, we already have a cross to bear; so don't place extra unneeded weight upon your cross. The Apostle Paul illustrates to us the difficulties of being a "human" Christian. In Romans the seventh chapter, he says that the good that he knows that he is supposed to do, he sometimes find it difficult to do, and the wrong that he knows that he is not supposed to do, he finds himself easily doing.

All the Apostle Paul was trying to tell us is that even though he is an Apostle, he is still human, and suffer with human problems.

Don't be so quick to look down on a saint that has fallen; we're not saved by works. We're saved by grace!

Perhaps you have fallen, but you can get up. It is not the fall that most concerns our Heavenly Father; it is what you do after you've fallen. We should always try to be the best person that we can be, and show the world Christ through our living.

Christians are suppose to be the most forgiving, and loving people on the planet, for the supreme God of the universe saved them even when they were unworthy and unfit to be saved.

So, be quick to get up after you've fallen, or been knocked down; and when you get up, reach back and help somebody else up!!!

Keep Trying To Fly

For Thanksgiving, I went home to visit my mother; while there, I went to the beach where I had gone many many times when I was just a boy growing up there. I stood on the shore and watched a flock of seagulls just feet away from me.

Suddenly, they all started to fly away, but seemed to be caught in a contrary draft of wind. They were only several feet from me, and I watched them flap their wings desperately trying to move forward, but to no avail. They just stayed in that on place. All of them were flapping and crying out, but going no where-the wind was simply too strong.

After a few moments, they all just landed on the beach in unison, and waited for the hard current to shift; but, there was on seagull that remained in the air; he kept flapping, kept screaming out, and like the others, he too didn't go anywhere; but he just wouldn't quit. I just kept looking at him.

I thought to myself, "When is this dumb bird going to quit like the rest?" He just kept on flapping; kept on screaming, but going nowhere. Even the seagulls on the ground seemed to be looking up at him and thinking like I was, "When is that dumb bird going to give up and come down?"

Just when I had picked up a sea shell to toss at him to make him come down, the wind shifted, and off he soared like a rocket. He never had to flap his wings for a long time; he just road that current until I could see him no more . . . . Soon, the other seagulls, that were on the ground took to the air, but still had to fly against contrary winds.

I thought to myself; that is just like life is as we attempt to walk by faith. Contrary winds are always blowing, and it is so much easier to just give up and join the rest of the quitters, and doubters, and faithless folks who are sitting around waiting passively for the winds to shift their way; waiting for

someone to give them a hand out; waiting for somebody else to change things for them; but, we must be like that seagull that had to fly by himself because he refused to quit . . . . flying and screaming . . . . flying and screaming . . . .

You might have to cry sometimes, but don't you dare land; you might have to scream by yourself, but don't you dare land; others might look at you and call you dumb, stupid, senseless, crazy, but don't you dare land.

If you keep flying, keep praying, keep yelling out for God, he will cause the contrary winds in your life to shift, and you too will be able to ride those new winds to greater heights while those quitters, and haters, and doubters, and complainers, and faithless folks are still where they have always been-complaining about the contrary winds, and still waiting on somebody to help them out.

No matter what, you stay the course!

Yes, sometimes it is difficult, but keep flying because one day very soon, your winds are going to shift and shoot you forth to make up for all the toiling that you have had to endure!

An Old Door

An F5 tornado had torn through a neighborhood in Birmingham, while trying to do whatever we could to give some help to those people that were hit the hardest by the tornado, I ran into an old lady that was sitting on what was left of the front porch of her house.

She was just smiling and thanking God for sparing her life. Her house had been blown away. She only had the clothes on her back; all of her material goods lay destroyed amidst the rumble everywhere.

She said that God used an old door to protect her . . . "God wouldn't let the devil come through that old door." She kept on saying.

I thought of how many times perhaps God had taken something that others thought was no good, and saved somebody with it.

After talking to the old lady, and having prayer with her, I said to myself that we ought to be willing to become one of God's old doors, and allow him to save somebody through us.

Be God's old door, and watch him deliver somebody through you

A Black Man

I must forge forth and be a man
And be all that I can
Pressing my history in the sand
Each day starting all over again

A BLACK MAN

They refuse to see me
Or recognize me
And acknowledge that I am free
I am a man too hued from God's tree

A BLACK MAN

Though my skin has been burned by the sun
And many have tossed me aside like I am done
And laugh at me just for fun
Or acted like brains, I have none

A BLACK MAN

I acted like I didn't hear the things you said
Or see my many sons you bled
And feel the pain when you forced
my woman your son to bred
I was living but dead

A BLACK MAN

My fate many have tried to foretell
Saying that I am something less than a male
But still I stand firm as my actions yell
Of how much of a man I excel

A BLACK MAN

High is my bail
To keep me in jail
They hope that even my race will fail
But still onward I sail
For I too have something to tell

A BLACK MAN

The laws are loaded
With paragraphs being quoted
Of how to keep me empty and bloated
With every day crimes that is noted

A BLACK MAN

Repeatedly I am knocked down
Still I get back up without even a frown
For I know that in me is a king who wears a crown
Ready to foster a better world right down to my single town

A BLACK MAN

And though I've been marred and beaten
I am still proud of my black skin
For the sun took special notice of me and my kin
More than the lighter others that he
looked on every now and then
Making some of us a colorful blend

A BLACK MAN

Proud am I
for though they beat me all I can do is die
and even then the king in me shall rise high
while praying for them without even a sigh
And bid my friends my enemies and
this troubled world good bye

A BLACK MAN

Broken Wings

My wings be broken
So my flying is but a token
And all of my dreams are choken
By too few wonderful things spoken

But I'll still try to fly
Until I die
And have no further strength to try

Nay sayers stand and look at me and cry
Of how futile it is for me to try
To fly and fly and fly
With wings so broken and dry

So patch me up here and stitch my broken wing there
That I might find room to fare
And walk boldly and even dare
To fight out of my toils of daily nightmare

My wings are broken but still please wind get under my feet
And lift me high above the troubles I meet
And fare me till it is my feat
To occupy the heavens in a glorious seat
Before they drape me under the white mortician sheet

Ambitions aching my very joints
So to the heavens I point
There where flying the eagles learnt

My wings are broke
But still I help folk
For others to soak
Of success unbroke

Though my wings are broken but it doesn't stop me
For I've learned to fly without wings on me
And taste the freedom that be
From flying and flying ever so free
Even with broken wings on me

My wings are broken

Enemy

Oh but my greatest enemy
Is oh so easy for me to see
For daily from the mirror he stands and stare back at me
Laughing at how frail and weak I can be

If I could just get my enemy inside
To yield and calmly abide
While forever resting inside
Sometimes resurrecting some of my
old demons who had died
And dominating the good in me that find it hard to reside

Often I hope and joyously dream
But inside he makes me frighten and scream
Afraid of people who are never as they seem
Making me forget I am a part of my master's redeemed

Those that were closes to me
Helped strengthen my enemy
Living inside of me
For they fed him things that he should be
And what he should see

Because my real enemy was blind to me
For daily I failed to see
What he was doing to me
Robbing me of the king that I should be

All my life in the midst of strife he told me who I am
Defeated deflated nothing in my mind my enemy rammed
Reinforcing me to remain apart of the damned

But now I recognize him inside of me
My real enemy
That I must change if I am to be free
And acquire all the riches the master stored up just for me

So I'll hush him up when he speaks out of term
And help him to learn
To cast aside defeat and victory confirm
Until my inside and my outside become one in turn
Then I'll constantly celebrate and not mourn

My Lover Still

The other day I heard of your new lover's feel
And I be not surprised that you're in my heart still
For love that plunges the heart is yet hard to kill
Desperately I try to hide my emotions
for you still rock and reel

I've accepted we are through for ever
But secretly in my heart you'll always be my lover
Nightly coming to me in secret dreams under my cover
My forever sweet grasping lover

Privately in my closet I weep for you
As lovers often do
Hoping the best for you
Even though we be through

Dearest I hope that your new love will treat you right
And you'll not have to fuss and fight
All through the availing night
I pray they help you achieve your born plight

In my heart where nobody sees you're still mine
On the outside I act as though I am fine
Every now and then imagining your
sweet fragrance as a young pine
Sipping on our old love like aged wine

Though you're not here, I feel you lying
beside me in the morning light
I imagine those morning eyes so bright
Pushing aside my pending fright
Until all is right
I caress and kiss with gentle morning bites
Filled with a heart that's so bright

I pretend I don't see you when you pass bye
All I can do is sigh
And ponder and wonder why
Did our hearts have to say good bye

Now somebody else fill the shoes that I once wore
And perhaps mend the heart that I once tore
Closing the door to your heart that I can enter no more
But still you are in my heart for sure

Oh but night after night I cry
Because my heart just refuse to finally say bye bye
To the heart that was suppose to be mine until I die

To others I pretend like I no longer care
But during my lonely secret nights I can hardly bare
Sitting in my darken room in my lonely chair
Wondering how you fair

Do you secretly miss me as much as I secretly miss you
Or have you just moved on and completely
accepted that we're through
And gave lips that were once mine to a new Boo
Our once love gone as yesterdays morning dew

So now I must wipe my tears and get up
And act like I am alright and nothing
amidst or file is in my cup
But every day this ole heart that's still yours almost erupt
From thoughts of hope that one day again we will sup

Proverbs

-The words that men concentrate to say is of little value
But the words that men speak casually matters most

-Free food will never save a starving man

-Worry about nothing, and do not despair
because at the end, we all die
The good, the bad, the holy, the evil, the
lover, and the hater, they all journey
Down the same road called death-
thus, we live among the dieing

-Be merry for tomorrow we die; it matters not
what you have come to have, or what and
Who you must leave behind; we all die in the end

-Truth is but measured word coming from a lying tongue

-Because they walk with you and laugh
with you doesn't mean that they will
fight with you or for you

-Every man has his own price

-Because they are by your side
Does not mean that they are on your side

-We live among the dieing
On our way to die to be among the living

-If your words are not solid
Your actions are but watery at best

-You can never grasp your future
If you constantly hold your past in your present

Yesterday's Gone

Yesterday is gone and tomorrow has not come
Yet I remember where I come from
Always striving to gain some
Right down to the day I am done

Forgiving those from my yesterday
Fearing that I might unknowingly stray away
From the laws my Father lay
And the things that he already say

Yesterday is gone but I hurt still
Trying to control my will
Of carrying yesterdays hurtful stuff still
And hoping those yesterday's pains I'll cease to feel

I'll make better today
For today will very soon be yesterday
Then I shall say I am good today because of yesterday
My todays are too fastly becoming my yesterday

Your Creation

What I am you made me
What I think you taught me
How I act you trained me
And my temper you gave me

Now you stress about me
Not wanting or liking what you created in me

You hate your creation
So you try to keep me in incarceration
While you design my annihilation
Without any humane reservation

You sit in deep meditation
Coming up with new legislation
To legally write me a new citation
Hoping to put me back in incarceration

Me and my brothers you constantly profile
Making us feel unclean and defiled
Less than even a child
While we rest at the top of your criminal file

Beaten but not defeated
For my dreams cannot be deleted
While you walk around being conceited
Hoping that my ancestor's slavery will be repeated

Knocked down but not knocked out
Cause dream filling is what I am about
And though I might have some fears and doubt
Still I search for another successful route
Instead of sitting around and just pout

Its time for me to create a new me
And I shall decide what I am to be
For freedom is not free
Just as some seeing men fail to see

I'll look at me
And have my tongue to release me
And commission my brain to direct me
And my body to obey me
As I blossom into the successful new me
That I was supposed to be

Broken Heart

Why won't my heart just leave me alone
Knowing full well that that relationship is gone

Why won't it just leave me alone
And let me move on

Your smile haunts me
Your kiss taunts me
Your gentle touch flaunts me

Oh miserable soul am I
For inwardly I just cry
While to others I blatantly lie
Of how I am over you but inside daily I die

Oh god why won't does old feeling just die
And allow me to soar high
In new relationships to fly
But I just can't forever bid you good bye

I refuse to admit it but you are a part of me
Buried deep down inside of me
Where others cannot see
The me
That's still deeply into you and cannot be completely free

Secretly I ask others how you are doing
and hope that you're alright
I should surrender and yield to this constant heart fight

I wonder if I'll ever completely be over you
But I don't know if I really want to

I cherish the little bit of you that's still in me
The part of you that's still mine that hasn't gotten free of me
My burning yearning flesh for you, you cannot see
And I guess that is good for me
For you might think less of me
Seeing that you have freed yourself from me

Still I love you even though I don't want to
I shall never love another like I love you
Even though we are through
And you have replaced me with another Boo

They say that it is better to have loved and lost
But oh how much does past love cost
For it leaves your heart under a constant frost
And your feeling of intimacy with others you just toss

But still this crazy heart of mine won't let me move on
I love you still
Outwardly I smile while inwardly I cry
And though it has been awhile
My heart is broken still

My Ass Outside

I rode up today on my ass
Not in my car cause it's cheaper than gas
And though it doesn't possess all that pizzazz
It's still but my precious ass
So when you talk about me and my faults and say I won't last

Just walk outside and kiss my Ass

In this race I might come in last
But there be some that started out but didn't last
And though sometimes I enjoy a little jazz
Don't cast me aside and say I am past
So when you talk about my faults and say I faded fast

Just walk outside and kiss my Ass

Though it only eats grass
And never run as a horse, never that fast
But it's still my ass
Only eating simple god grown grass
So when you talk about my faults and a mess I've amassed

Just walk outside and kiss my Ass

Like fishing for big mouth bass
And fighting with him till no more strength he has
My enemies attack me, but they won't last
Cause I've learned to be stubborn just like my Ass
So when you talk about my faults and say of me sin blast

Just walk outside and kiss my Ass

Everywhere I go I take my Ass
Because somebody always wants to ride my Ass
Cause its cheaper than gas
So when you talk about my faults and my past

Just walk outside and kiss my Ass

For whatever reason you might want to ride my ass
Just know for sure your ride won't last
Cause after all, it's still my Ass
And all my troubles always soon past
So when you talk about my faults and say out I've been cast

Just walk outside and kiss my Ass

Akeam Simmons

Somebody To Love Me

You always need somebody to love you
And be in love with you
To help you get through
The daily storms that you have to

Someone to say I love you
Even after the awful things that you do
And just living has made your days blue
Someone to say you're still their Boo

You still need somebody to love you
When a change is long over due
But you're still just you
Covered in yesterday's hurt like morning dew

Somebody to love you when the chips are down
And you sadder than a tearful clown
Where no friends to be found
You just day by day just hanging around

You need somebody to love you when you feel loveless
When you are not your best
Over and over again you fail life's test
And your life has become one big mess

You need someone to love you
Cause love will always bring love to you
Matters not what your ethnic is-white, black, or Jew
Love will help you outgrow the old hindering you
The you, you should have long ago slew

So take not for granted those that love you
And the one that's in love with you
You need love to help you get through
The storms that life blew
To guide you to your purpose designed just for you

Letter To My Daddy

Thought I'd write to you
Cause I never see you
Mama says you're too busy doing you
But whose going to help mama do
me while you are doing you

You busy trying to be a G
Does that mean you cant take time for me
And help mama raise me
To grow up to see
And be the adult I am supposed to be

I wanted you to tuck me in at night
And tell me that I'll be alright
Fighting some of the same demons that you fight
Family demons that causes our confusing midnight

I hear mama crying at night
Trying to hide her tears from me so I won't fright
Of things she endure that's not right
Hoping to give me a better plight
And put some hope in my sight

But why you leave us
Or were you ever with us
Don't you care about us
Or are we just a wondering piece of dust
That you accident over heaping lust

I see you sometimes on the street
And wish with all my might that you would come and meet
With me the child you fail to see
I am just a little you that's trying to be

I look in the mirror and I see you looking back at me
So why you try to deny me
Even a blind man can see that you created me
But I don't want to be another G
Like you on the way to the graveyard early

Dear daddy even though I don't want to
I still love you just as parent's children often do
Hoping that someday the best will come out of you
And you'll realize that I am yours too
Along with your other children you overlook too

The Melting Snow

Alone I stare through my cold window seal
Trying to forget and forge ahead from the deepen pain I feel
Hoping my emotions will be still
And afford me a time to just heal

Outside the snow is melting and lazily
falling upon the frozen ground
Inside the fire place crackles, still by lonely tears I am bound
Nothing in the melting snow eases me to lie down
And rest for a while from peace I've yet found

Melting Melting forever still
Oh broken heart of yester years
From winter's darken icy fears
Howling through snow melodies only I hear

Collecting upon the ground in white velvety heaps
Melting faster than one can keep
My emotions shouldn't be so deep
And melt away like the snow's heap

Oh that I would find the peace of sleep
That comes during winter's creep
And nearly flat lines my heart without even a beat
There where ghostly souls weep
Of time they fail to reap

Now I sit in the warmth of my home alone
Watching the snow melt and drip slowly as an ice cream cone
Flakes of snow from heaven flown

Now I know that I shall be alright
For just as the sun and snow forever fight
My heart shall mend anew through this night
And bring me fresh new rights
Just as the fleeting snow lights
Of colors yet so bright

From Hell I Come

I raised myself
Bathed myself
Taught myself
Fought myself

The ancients were my forever unyielding school masters
Been there
Done that
Seen that

My destiny is ever before me
My failures are ever behind me
My love is ever inside me
My God is ever upon me

Now is then
And then is now
I evolve from then
To conquer now

Yesterday is always behind me
Today is always within me
Tomorrow is always resting at my thresh hold
Time is my constant companion friend

I am carried about by faith
Riding on the wings of hope
My shield is heaps of charity
My weapons be need and passion

My enemy is ignorance
My foe is stupidity
That which weakens me is hate
That which strengthens me comes
from the breath of my God

Delayed but not denied
For delay simply preps me for destiny
I am come forth to go forth
And conquer the conquerable

My mother is love
My father is faith
My siblings are wind, earth, fire, and rain
I am the best of my Father's children

Up from hell I come
Unwavering willing and ready
Blessed and cursed
My feet implanted on victory's soil

Up from hell I come
With an unquenchable thirst
And an endless appetite
To know
And be known

Up from hell I come
Wearing whelps of pain in my bosom
But refusing to be broken
Even amidst brokenness

Up from hell I come
Riding upon heaven's shore
Of streets of gold
And gates of pearls

Up from hell I come
Up from hell I come
Up from hell I come

Phantom Lover

Another night I fill my pillow with lonely tears
Holding my pillow close upon my breast
Wishing that it was you; wishing that it was your touch
Your hand that eased the tears from my face

I hasten that the angel of sleep would find my bed
For after I slumber upon my bed
You come with kisses ever so sweet
With love ever so deep
That I cannot but yield my passion starved flesh to you

We laugh and play upon my bed
And forge memories of love and happiness unfeigned
Your touch, oh your touch
You take my breath away

Tears ease from my eyes
As dawn slowly creeps through my window seal
Knowing full well that you must take your leave
I weep
Your touch vanishes in a moment

I open my eyes
Again tears creep upon my pillow
As my heart bellows of last night
A night filled with passion and love

A smile smothers my face
For I know that another night is just beyond the horizon
Where I shall leap into your arms again
And kiss the night away
As I hope you shall leave my dreams
And step out of my nights and fill my days

But we must not fret for it is all we have right now
Memories of last night
In our dreams of passion so sweet
With days yearning for night to come
When the angel of sleep ushers you to my bed again

The Beast In Me

Fighting and fighting and raging deep in me
Like the perfect storm that refuse to cease
The beast inside of me
Torments me to let him free

Every time I hurt he screams of agony
Shaking every fiber inside of me
Wanting to fight the battles I refuse to see
And rescue me from my every enemy

Little rest for real
So hard for me to stand still
For the beast in me rocks and reels
Refusing to rest or be steal

Every man's a liar
Every woman's a conniver
I am consumed by stickers and briars
While everyone is simply a complier

I moan a song to set me free
And ease the beast inside of me
Where peace and torment fights bitterly
Raging the war for the best of me

Oh silent night
Filled with fright
From the beast inside of me that I tire to fight
Almost depleting my might

Silly women and silly men
Refuse to let me alone to mend
These bitter emotions I contend
Hoping to ease my beast within

Inside of me he rage and rage until little strength left
Because of silly old men whose just stuck on self
With little or no spiritual depth
And no conscious wealth

But I'll fight with the beast in me
Until my eyes close the last time and refuse to see
And every day I'll force the best in
me to fight the beast in me

Is There A Ghetto In Heaven

Lord I hope there is no ghetto in heaven
Divided and separated my race creed and color
I've gone through much of that on earth; where
the color of my skin dictated my worth
Where I got substandard food, and substandard
education, and substandard rights

My bones are weary and tired of fighting for
equal rights and holding signs of Help Me
Don't want to do that on the other side in Heaven
I don't want substandard wings and a crooked
halo that came from the better section

In Heaven, I don't want to live in a shack
while others live in a Mansion
Don't want streets paved with black tar
While the other section are paved with gold
I want to be just another angel in heaven
who's just like all the others up there

Is there a ghetto in heaven
Should I even ask
But I wonder where those mean men go to
Or those caring liberals that just kept silent amidst my pain

Will they escort me to a section of heaven
where others look like me
With barred windows and locked doors
Will heaven have shot houses and decrepit shacks
With a liquor store on every other corner

Akeam Simmons

Is there a ghetto in heaven

No there is no ghetto in heaven
I'll only have to live in hell once
The color of my skin will only matter here
Where mean men do dwell and fear

God is too faithful
Too loving
To hide me or store me in some wretched ghetto in heaven
No that's why he created a hell cause
there is no ghetto in heaven

So now
I'll smile when I look through the burglar bars
I'll smile when the wind blows through
the cracks of my shack
I'll smile when they come into my neighborhood
and arrest me for being black
I'll smile when I stumble over the pot holes in my street
Heaven is a ghettoless place
Where angels do fly
And the throne of God do rest

In heaven
I'll be amongst the angelic community
Where color doesn't matter
And my neighborhood is just that
My angelic neighborhood

No liquor stores
No burglar bars
No fallen down shacks
No crooked policing angels

Is there a ghetto in heaven
No cause God will pull me out of the ghetto
And let me rest in heaven in his bosom for all eternity
While he sooths my wombs
Afflicted upon me in earth's ghetto

Akeam Simmons

Deserted Heart

Here I go again
Like fleeting sugar from withering stalks of cane
I wrench and jeer my brain
Trying desperately to explain
My broken heart's disdain

Here I sit alone again . . . . again
You promised to never leave me or cause me such pain
But nightly my tears soak my pillow like stormy rain
While I struggle with my self respect to maintain

But who am I to blame
I must sternly proclaim
I bellow I must be insane
To allow my heart over and over again to be slain

I can't much blame you
For if I could I would leave me too
All of my issues and mess through and through
Old relationships resting on me like morning dew

I am broken into pieces and need putting back together
So come unknown lover mend me and make me better
And we'll become one and love forever
Bending but not breaking like a strong piece of leather

I know that one day soon
I'll laugh again under the glowing moon
And love a blossom again like flowers in June
Then my lover will chase away my hearts gloom

Oh kiss me till the morning come
My body conquered exhausted still I yearn some
Hold me till my heart is no longer numb
And my reasoning of love is no longer dumb

Take me lead me where a kiss is not merely a kiss
But warm lips filled with passion and bliss
Where mouths lock together with moaning and hiss
From lover's nights long missed

The Other Side Of Through

My heart broken
I am going through
Through heart break
Through emotional blackness
Through long days and black nights
Through constant midnights and few sun lights
Through mourning and weeping
Through tears and mourning
Through isolated loneliness
Through dieing in living
Through let downs and disappointments
Through desertions and jealousies
Through fearful friends and fearless enemies
Through ups and downs
Through loveless relationships
Through dire relationships
Through fleeting passion
Through dry kisses and hollow holding

I am going through
But I know that there is the other side of through
When I am through with through
Where joys is on the other side of through
Where love and passion and kisses and
holding is on the other side of through

I weep tonight cause I am going through
But too I joy tonight cause I know there
is the other side of through
Where roses blossom amidst lilies
Where kisses are filled with passion
Where holding never cease
And sweet cuddling is my norm
accompanies by gentle touches

The other side of going through
Is a place of laughter and big broad smiles
And warm glistening eyes

So when I am going through
I am never overly saddened cause there
is another side to my through
A side to when I shall laugh again and smile again
And love again
And feel the warm touch of my lover

An Old Fool

Nothing like an old fool
For they chase women and men that
they know they can't have
And dress today out of yesterday
Whose body has changed and eased into a new day

Nothing like an old fool
That's chasing their youth and denying their age
Who refuse to see what's looking back at them in the mirror
And hair color has become their secret obvious friend

Nothing like an old fool
Who chases butter and waists cheddar
And sees no further than what he sees
Or reach no further than his grasp

Nothing like an old fool
Whose days are ushered in by guarded hangovers
And gathering booty for next night's wasting loot
For a moment's pleasure with uncaring
stilettos or shiny boots

Nothing like an old fool
That utters age ain't nothing but a number
But still tries desperately to hide the number
Who enlarge the pockets of vanity stores
And wait endlessly at cosmetic counters

Nothing like an old fool
That party with their children
And hang out with babies struggling with their own youth
Analgesics are their constant friend
That cover up slow starts and unexplained stops

Nothing like an old fool
That spends most of their labored money on botox
And increasing their breast or enlarging their fertilizers
Who fail to love themselves for who they are
But measure their self worth by Hollywood's commercials

Nothing like an old fool
That use to be an old fool
That appreciates his blessings of longevity
And opportunities to help mold and shape a new generation
That's thankful for the face that's staring
back at them in the mirror
Whose lap is grandchildren's favorite place
And whose arms are grandbabies
shields from the world's hurt

Nothing like an old fool
That use to be an old fool
For they celebrate seeing another sunrise
And are thankful to stare up in the night's sky
And watch the stars and heavenly host sparkle in the sky
Who appreciates another day's journey
And are thankful to their God
For looking beyond their many varied faults
And sustaining them anyhow and blessed them
Even when they didn't deserve to be

Nothing like an old fool
That use to be an old fool
That now salvages old friends and new friendships
And harbor not hate or avenges in their heart
Who constantly labor at love and are quick to forgive
And measure themselves by the measure of the almighty

Nothing like an old fool
That's been redeemed from the pains of being an old fool
Who ushers in wisdom to quickly pour out to others
That's thirsty and hungry and looking
for the right path of life
They cherish their children and grand babies
Realizing full well that they are an extended part of them

Nothing like an old fool
That's learned to be an old wise person
Fill with good advice about proper living
And real joy and happiness
Appreciating who you are and what you are
And gleaning the times of where you are

Nothing like an old fool
That is now a wise

Lonely Tears

Here I go again crying to myself about myself
Filled with pain and loneliness and ill health
I thrust my hurt upon my wavering emotional shelf
And pray my heart flee this broken death
Like a labored thief without theft
My soul silent and partly deaf
While I measure myself by myself

Only Fools Fall In Love

Only fools fall in love

For they break their own heart
They become blind and fail to see
And sometimes don't even want to see
And ever believes in the impossibility being possible

Only fools fall in love

For they will see a prince in a frog
And give up everything for nothing
Hoping to make a dog a man
And turn a snake into a Lady

Only fools fall in love

For they thrust themselves through with pain
And reason their hurt faults of theirs
Weeping of yesterday and hopes of tomorrow
Hoping to satisfy their lust for love

Only fools fall in love

For they venture where brave men fear to go
And leap into the dark side in hopes of love
Every day is spent hoping
While every night is spent in the grips of lonely passion

Only fools fall in love

But oh how I seek to become the fool
And find another fool drawn to me
Where two fools can walk hand in hand
Amidst smiles of splendor
While on lookers wreak to be fools just like us

Proverbs

-Fame and beauty are but sisters
For they are forever fleeting and failing

-An army with too many leaders
Will soon fail

-The folly of leadership
Is seeking a friendly face

—Be not deceived by a smile
For it is merely a frown turned up side down

—If you must fight
Fight with all your might

—If you must lose
Lose only after having done everything to win

—Let not slumber find your eyes
While your enemy lurks

—Happy is the woman who captures the heart of a man
For her burdens shall be lightened

—If you have to ask your woman can you do it
You probably don't need to do it

—When a man has to ask his woman's permission
He is stripped of his manhood
He has become but a grown child

—A woman will never love a man she cannot respect
And she will not continue to love a
man who she has lost respect

—Experience is not always the best Teacher
Although by far it is a very good Teacher

—Sex is a drug
That makes wise men fools
And fills fools full of folly

—Even while you sleep
Your woman thinks the trick

—For she knows that you cannot miss
That for which you cannot measure

—It is a bad wind that never changes

—Never betray the one you share the cup with

—Flee death with all your might
But know full well that you can never out run death
For it will soon find you where ever you are

—Youth is folly
For it tricks its carrier into foolishness

—To be old is to be blessed of the Lord

—A woman's eyes will always unveil the truth

—Man is but a vain deceiver

—A man's words will deceive you
But his tracks cannot
Follow his tracks and there you will find the real man

—Religion is often the birth place of fools
And gives rise to foolishness
Where greed, hate, and profanity is covered up by order

—Never allow your flesh to make decisions for your heart
For in the end, misery shall be your companion friend

—Seek not the counsel of a fool

—Beware of the ambitious man
For he is nobodies friend

—If you seek the easiest way to do a
lot of labor in a short time
Assign the labor to a lazy man

—All men are but liars
Therefore you must search for the truth

—Beauty is but a deceiver
For it covers ugliness, filth, and pain

—He that makes decisions while in bed with a woman
If the chief of fools

—In times of trial
A man will always return to where he is most comfortable

—Failure is fuel for success

Craps

My turn again to roll the dice
I shake and toss
Already knowing the likelihood of duce ones or snake eyes
But I heave the toss anyhow

Hoping for better this time
Knowing already that the dice is going to do
What the dice has always done
The height of hope is to stay in the game
And hope nobody sees how much I've lost

I peer into the eyes of the other foolish players
Trying to make something of nothing
Transformed to become little more than thieves
Hoping to steal another's man's purse

I toss
For if I toss not there is no chance of a win
They roll across the velvety table like two scrambling mice
Cheers around me thunder hoping for what the dice will do

They stop 11
I breathed with exhilaration
Another chance to roll again
Not knowing if I might win or lose
But still I must roll

And roll
And roll
And roll
And roll

If I roll not
There is no chance of win
The only way to win is to roll
If I am in the game I must roll
And every once in a while the dice will favor me

The bystanders and onlookers
Will never feel the thrill of the dice
For I must feel the hardness of the dice in my sweaty hands
And sit upon hope and despair of win or lost

At the end of the night
I exit feeling good that I was a player
Sometimes winning
Sometimes losing
But still I played the game
While bystanders envied me when I won
And lamented me when I lost

I played when I could
So at the end of the night
I know full well that I was a player
Taking chances
Winning and losing
But still playing

And when tomorrow comes
I will play some more
Winning some and losing some
But still I'll play
Cause the only way to win sometimes
Is I got to be one of the players
For bystanders and onlookers never have the chance to win

Heaven's Door

Porclaius lay upon the warm white sands, awakened by the pounding waves of the restless sea. The golden sun glistened and beat steadily upon his bronze muscular body.

He staggered to his feet; his head swirling; his thoughts racing like an out of control falling plane dashing thunderously towards the ground. He rubbed his hands over his bald head, and wiped the rolling sweat leaping down his brow. He looked all around to see what he could see of where he was, or even how he got there. Palm trees swayed back and forth, dancing from the gentle strength of the soft blowing east wind.

He turned and began to walk towards the sweltering tree lines of the beach-looking for any signs of human life. Colorful birds streaked across the never ending sky, while white seagulls screamed and rode the whistling wind that shifted over the deep blue sea.

Porclaius walked through the forest for what seemed like hours-every step leading him farther away from the seashore—Still no signs of human life anywhere. Where is this place? He thought to himself. He grabbed a large leaf from one of the green leaning trees, and wrapped it around his waist-covering his nakedness.

He walked and walked, endlessly, until gradually easing upon a whispering waterfalls sliding down a verdant hill side. Dropping to his knees, he slurped big gulps of water—dipping his hand in the water then lifting it to his mouth.

Quickly he jerked around, trying to see from whence came the soft giggles behind him. He stumbled and landed upon his butt.

Three very pretty sun bathed young ladies giggled even harder at his falling.

"What . . . . what . . . . where . . . . where am I?" Porclaius stuttered. "Who are you?"

The young ladies just giggled with their hands over their mouths as they stared at Porclaius and whispered to each other.

He leaped to his feet. "Where is this place? What's it called?" He asked as he took a few steps towards them.

Suddenly, they dropped their hands, and velvety white wings sprang up from behind them; huge wings, with a ten foot span on either side stretched out peering into the heavens. Though their giggling had ceased, they smile broadly at Porclaius as they hovered a few feet from the ground—Their bodies gloriously sculptured and naked with only a satin piece of cloth covering their breast and their waist.

Porclaius staggered a few steps backwards in utter amazement. He tried desperately to say something, but words refuse to leap from his lips.

They eased a few more feet into the air; still smiling broadly at Porclaius. They whispered something to each other, and then began to fly slowly backwards as the stared at Proclaius.

"No, wait!" Porclaius proclaimed.

They stopped in midair, wings still fluttering like a Humming bird.

"Who are you? What are you? Where am I?" He continued to ask; now walking slowly towards them.

Again, they snickered, then turned and flew slowly off in the distance. Porclaius followed them; walking briskly through thickets of brush while being slapped here and there by branches. He refused to take his eyes off of them.

The girls peered back at him every now and then, still smiling as they went.

What is this place? He thought to himself; and how did I get here? He continued following as fast as he could. The girls started flying a little faster; broadening the distance between them and Porclaius.

Suddenly, he burst forth from the edge of the forest. Porclaius stopped in his tracks as he gazed at the girls flying up over the towering golden wall-glistening like the sun in noon day. His mouth fell open as he took a few steps forward. The doors of the golden gate began to slowly ease open.

Porclaius staggered backwards-not knowing what to expect.

A man with a glowing countenance and a long white beard that stretched to his chest looked hard at Porclaius.

"Saint . . . . Saint . . . . Saint Peter?" Porclaius stumbled.

"What? Please, I wish." The man with the long white beard said casually as he waved his hand at Porclaius to come closer. "No, Saint Peter is in the middle court; quite a distance from here. This is the last outer court; once you cross here, there is no going back."

"And where is Here?" Porclaius said as he pointed his slender finger at the golden gate surrounding something.

"You've got to be the dumbest fellow in the universe if you can't even guess what this place is." The old man snickered as he spoke softly to Porclaius.

"I don't like guessing."

"Heaven, if you just got to know," said the man waving his hand behind him at the golden gates.

"You mean um dead?"

"Well, kind of, sort of."

"What you mean kind of, sort of? Um either dead or um not." Porclaius reasoned.

"Well, it's not that cut and dry for folk like you."

"What you mean, folk like me?" Porclaius took a few more steps closer to the white bearded man.

"Remember, once you cross this threshing, there is no turning back." He pointed down at the threshing floor as he spoke.

Porclaius quickly stepped a couple of feet back.

"You're in, what we call up here, Bodevah. It's the folk that live outside the Gate; they're not ready to come in, but they're not ready to return to earth. Some have been up here for a few days-which equals to a few years of your earthly time."

People, men, women, and children, began to walk out of the forest and gather around Porclaius as he spoke to the man with the white beard
He turned and began to walk back into the inner courts—the glistening golden Gate slowly followed him, as if pushed by an invisible hand, as he walked.

"No, wait!" Porclaius took a few steps forward as he yelled out.

"Remember, once you cross the threshing there is no going back."

Porclaius stopped in his tracks, and stepped backwards.

"The others will speak to you of your state. I shall return in a few days. Perhaps then, you shall have made up your mind. You earthlings are so confused most times. He yelled back without turning around, as the last few steps of the golden doors shut with an echoing boom.

"But I thought you said a few days is like a few years on earth!" Porclaius yelled after him.

"Oh it is dear sir; not Like, it is dear sir . . . . It is." The soft voice of a lady whispered towards him; she stepped forward and put out her hand to shake. "Oh, excuse me, I am Amelia . . . . Amelia Earhart."

"What! No way!" Porclaius exclaimed.

A small crowd had gathered around Porclaius by now. They escorted him back to their small village as the talked.

"How long do you think that you've been here now?" One of the men asked Porclaius.

"A few hours." He responded.

"Ha, almost a year earth's time." The man whipped.

"I think it's been a little longer," another man yelled from the crowd.

"And, who might you be dear sir?" Porclaius asked the man.

"Um Jimmy Hoffa." The man snapped. "The one and only."

"Remember, everything here happens fast. Earth's time moves at a Snell's paste compared to up here," said Jimmy with a big smile.

That night, one of the young ladies came to Porclaius' hut, and they talked for most the night about everything and anything-they laughed and joked; and for a moment Proclaius forgot about where he was, and the thousands of questions he needed answered.

"We've been up all night, and yet I am not tired," said Porclaius as he rose to his feet and peered out of the hut at the rising sun.

"We never sleep here. We don't need it." She said.

"So, I've been up a year without sleet-huh?"

"Yea, almost."

"What is your name?"

"When you kissed me last night, you didn't ask my name."

"I was caught up in the moment, and your beauty overwhelmed me."

"I shall have a child in a few moments-your child."

"What!"

"Yes, it only takes an hours to conceive and deliver-which is a year our earth's time."

"But"

Before Porclaius could say another word, she bent over with labor pains. "Go get Amelia!"

"But"

"Pleaseeeeee!"

"Ok, Ok." Porclaius ran out of the hut, and saw Amelia walking briskly towards him.

"Good, good, come now she asks for you."

"What's wrong with Stacy?" Amelia said, walking right pass him headed for the hut.

"Stacy?"

"Yea Stacy . . . . What . . . . What's wrong with her?"

"You're not gone believe this, but she says that she is about to have a baby."

"Yea, I believe her. Remember earth time, it's been almost a year for you."

"But"

"Did you touch her?" Amelia snapped.

"Er . . . ah . . . ."
"Well, did you all copulate . . . . Well did you?"

"Yea, but, who gets pregnant and have the baby the same night?" Porclaius exclaimed nervously.

"Remember, you're not on earth. You all were in that hut most of the day and all the night. That's nearly a year in earth's time."

Two days had past, and Porclaius was still trying to get use to this new time that he was in. In a matter of hours, he watched his son grow from an infant into a toddler, and on to a two year old. In a couple of days, he had married Stacy, and now had a two year old son.

A loud ram's horn pierced the air. Everyone came out of their huts, and stopped what they were doing and rushed towards the Golden Gates. Stacy grabbed Porclaius and her little son's hand and hurriedly walked towards the Gate.

The Golden Gates quietly eased open. The man with the white beard stepped forward with a slight smile upon his face.

"No new arrivals this hour, but have any of you made up your minds—you want to cross over, go back to earth, or stay here in Bodevah a little longer, or until you have no other choice?"

Stacy looked up at Porclaius, and squeezed his hand-hoping that he wouldn't leave her and their son. Her breath's were short, her palms sweat, and beads of sweat gathered upon her forehead.

"And you, dear sir, Mr. Proclaius, our newest arrival; have you made up your mind yet" The man said as he looked sternly into Proclaius eyes.

Stacy's heart raced like galloping horses in her chest. She prayed; she hoped; she screamed inside that Proclaius wouldn't leave them.

"No, I think that I shall stay a little longer."

Stacy leaped into his arms and held him tightly with all of her might.

The old man glared at Stacy and the little toddler that looked just like Porclaius. "Can't stay here forever you know."

He gazed down at the little white book that was in his hand, and fumbled through it for a moment as the people grew deathly silent with anticipation.

"Ummmm . . . . Uh Oh . . . . I missed that one." He said, looking up from the book and into the crowd. "It is time for two of you."

Everybody moaned, and wondered who it was, as they looked among themselves. Somebody's family would be torn apart-some woman, some man, some child would be left in horrid grief.

"Ah . . . Mr. Harris, Howard Harris, and a Mr. Robert Levers."

Women screamed, while others cried aloud feeling their pain.

"NO . . . . NO . . . . NO . . . . I won't go!" Hollered one of the men, and began running back towards the village.

"Gosh, so much drama," said the man with the white beard. "Y'all know the rules. I explain them every time I come, and every time a new visitor comes . . . . Gosh, so much drama."

One of the men hugged his wife and his family, and then walked slowly towards the man with the white beard. His wife's eyes filled with tears, while his two little girls wept softly. He stopped, turned around and walked back to his wife and little girls.

"Y'all will be joining me very soon; just take care of mommy until we meet again." Again, he turned and walked to the man with the white beard.

"You ready?"

"Yea, ready as um a get." He turned, and waved again goodbye to his wife and children. "What's going to become of them? Will they have the choice to go back to earth, or heaven, or what?" He asked the man with the white beard.

"Your wife will have a choice, but your girls won't. They can't go to earth, for they were born in Bodevah-so, it's either heaven or Bodevah for them . . . . And knowing your wife, she will probably stay with them if she can; where ever they go."

The man with the white beard raised the white book high into the air and waved it around a few quick turns, and the man running towards the village disappeared in a whiff of wind as though he had never been.

"None of us stay here more that a year." Amelia whispered leaning into Porclaius ear.

"And how long is a year-earth time?"

"About 365 years more or less." Amelia said, looking back at the man with the white beard as he escorted his new resident beyond the Golden Gate.

"Where did the guy go that just disappeared?" Porclaius asked.

"Don't know; probably to hell or back to earth, but definitely not on the other side of those gates." Amelia said. "They don't take people that don't want to be there."

Porclaius had been in Bodevah now for nearly a week, which was nearly seven years in earth time. He had had two more children; a boy and another little girl. For him, life was good in Bodevah. He still couldn't remember where he had come from, so Bodevah was all that he knew.

Porclaius salvaged every moment with his family, for he never knew when would be his last moment with either of them-for the man with the white beard still came every so often and took someone while leaving a family broken and in tears. He loved his wife, and often played with his children. Every night, he and Stacy gazed into the black velvety sky and wondered among the twinkling stars.

"If we are ever parted, look up at the stars in the night sky, and you'll know that I am looking too; that way, we'll always have a connection," said Stacy, staring deeply into his eyes.

"I shall."

"No, for real, let's promise to do that.

"I shall. I promise." He smiled and pulled her closer to him.

He was happy and at peace with himself and others; happier than he had ever remembering being in his life.

The early morning breeze ran softly through the village carrying salt pebbles upon its wings. The golden sun rose lazily beyond the distant grey mountains while the last bit of a twinkling night's fire slowing simmered out. Stacy had slept cuddled in Porclaius arms, and dreamt the night away.

Suddenly, a loud ram's horn shattered the silence of peace that was ushering in the joy of a new day in Bodevah. Quickly, everyone jumped to their feet; racing to put on their clothes and meet the man with the white beard. Porclaius had been there a month now. His oldest daughter was now thirty years old, and his three other children were also young adults. The four of them held hands as they briskly walked through the forest towards the Golden Gate-knowing full well that this could very well be their last time together.

They stood nervously amongst the crowd as the man with the white beard eased from behind the Golden Gate.

He opened his white book, and slowly scrolled down the pages. "Ah yes . . . . It is time," he said.

A soft moan leaped from the crowd. "Who?" They all asked in Unisom.

"Mr. Porclaius, it is time." He said, staring into Porclaius eyes.

Stacy screamed, and fainted. Her three children tried to console her, even amidst tears screaming down their own faces.

The man with the white beard and the white book waited patiently while Porclaius turned to his wife and children to bid them farewell.

"You've got to be strong for our children Stacy, and you all must salvage the time that you now have with each other; for you never know when it shall be your last moments together. Hopefully, I'll see y'all again soon somewhere." He turned and tore himself from Stacy's arms and his children's loving grasp, and stepped up to the man with the white beard.

He raised the white book high into the air.

"Wait, you mean I am not going in there?" Porclaius pointed through the Golden Gates.

"No, it is not your time to go there."

"Then, where? I don't remember no other place."

The man with the white beard stuck the white book back into the air, and turned it quickly with a hard jerk back and forth.

Porclaius turned to Stacy and his children and waved goodbye-holding his own tears in his bosom. Quickly, he disappeared amongst a whiff of wind.

"Porclaius! Porclaius! I am glad you have awaken." A man's voice thundered into Porclaius ears. "You've been in a comma for a month. We thought that we were going to lose you."

Porclaius slowly looked around the room with wondering eyes, and slowly realized that he was in a hospital room. He burst into tears and wailed loudly as he pounded his fist upon the side of the hospital bed.

Porclaius spent the rest of his life morning for his wife and children that his father tried daily to convince him that he never had. Every night, he stared into the night at the twinkling stars hoping that Stacy and his children were watching the same stars too.

Proverbs

—That which has been shall always be
That which is has been
That which shall be has already been

-Joy and Sorrow
Are but kinfolk
Resting upon the shoulders of life's travelers

—Faith is the cure all medicine

—A good wife is priceless
For she is the salve that heals the afflicted

Another Me

Oh that I must grow old
That my hairs unveil my golden years
That my steps be not shorten
And my breaths be quickened like yester years

My children forsake me from time to time
When the rivers of my purse slows
And my hand of abundance withers to me
For my yes becomes maybes and my maybes becomes no

I salvage the thoughts of yesterday
When little feet raced across my floor
Getting into everything that little hands can get into
And going every place that little feet could carry them

My heart that pleads of love for love
That will love me for me all of me
The good the bad and the ugly
During my concealing nights and my revealing days

Wisdom knows my children and nurses them
But ignorance forsakes my children and
devours them while babies
I am wounded through and through from knowledge
For the more I see the blinder I wish to be

So many promises and promises
Forgotten yesterdays
And stolen tomorrows
But I salvage today and invest in right now

There be nothing more precious than purchased sense
And dieing yet not dieing
I be living and I live
For every moment is more precious than the last
And every breath is much sweeter than before

For there be always another me
From yesterday walking briskly into today
And leaping into the freshness of tomorrow

Another me to kiss the never ending sky
Another me to trot down the dust riddled roads of the future
Another me to lament for my brother
Another me to grab faith and trust by the groins
And move ever so steadily to what I want to be

Just evolving into ANOTHER ME

Can You Cry With Me

My tears lay upon my midnight pillow
Thrust upon me by long stilettos
With painted nails and sculptured toes
Laying down paths that every one goes

Will you cry with me just for tonight
And help me regain my self esteem before the night
To pull off this unwanted person I fight
Hoping praying and wishing that soon I'll be alright

Will you cry with me this one time
Help me overcome a body so fine
That I foolishly thought was mine
I fell for a painted face and hips that bind
Foolishly thinking this was one of a kind

Will you cry with me and chase away my loneliness
And allow me to become my best
Walking in the healthy wealthy blessed
Of surviving another stilettos test

Will you cry with me wailing liars that perform
To fight the fight to not conform
And become another whose blatantly deform
From heart aches that shouldn't be born

But cry with me tonight
And help me win my fight
I will be alright
I just need for us to cry tonight

I Miss Being Daddy

I miss holding you in my arms
And watching your little bright eyes look back at me
I miss you falling asleep on my chest
While I patted you softly in your back

I miss being daddy

I miss watching you learn to feed yourself
While making a mess everywhere
I miss seeing you put your clothe on backwards
And refusing help of any sort

I miss being daddy

I miss your big smile flashed upon me
When you beckoned for something you wanted from me
I miss hearing your little feet race across the floor
And you jumping into bed beside me

I miss being daddy

I miss wiping your tears away when you cry
And holding you tightly in my arms
I miss seeing your joy of the first day of school
And your first ride upon the school bus

I miss being daddy

I miss you helping me bake cookies
And wasting flour everywhere
I miss your little hugs

And your warm embraces trying
encourage my sometimes sad face

I miss being daddy

I miss your very first time trying to wash dishes
And getting just as much water on yourself as the dishes
I miss your good night stories
And early morning prayers

I miss being daddy

I miss your high school games
And standing on the sidelines cheering you on
I miss the excitement of your first prom
And nervously looking out the window
waiting your arrival home

I miss hearing your name called at high school graduation
And at the end of your college life
I miss watching you become a full adult
And going to your first new job

I miss being daddy

Even though you are grown now
And no longer lives at home
I still pray for you
And love you
Cause no matter how grown or old you become
You'll always be my little girl
And I will always be your daddy

A Prayer For The Nations

Dear Father God we come as humble as we know how; we give you all the praise, and all of the glory, and all majesty, and all honor, and all power, for we know that you have all power in your hand.

We thank you for all the blessings that you have bestowed upon us; blessings that we did not deserve, but because of your grace and goodness and mercy, you blessed us in-spite of ourselves, and for that Heavenly Father we want to say thank you.

We pray right now for our nations; at home and around the globe, for we are but one large community dependant upon each other. Father help us to see ourselves and where we fall short, and help us to be thankful for the many blessing that you have given us. We know that there are a lot of people around the globe that are not doing as well as us.

Bless the nations that they might seek you, and that our global leaders will seek your wisdom in leading the nations.

Where we have erred and gone after our own way, please forgive us, and give us a mind that seeks you and your wisdom.

Show us dear Father God that we need each other; we are no greater than the whole of us.

Give us a mind to unify, and become as one; that we might feel the need and pain of our brothers who are in nations that is less fortunate than us. Give us a mind to comfort the sick, feed the hungry, and to console those that are morning.

Give us peace in the midst of confusion; give us a mind to be at peace with all men, and be concerned about all men regardless of race, creed, color, or nationality.

Let us reach forth a hand of mercy, love, patients, and temperance unto our brothers at home and abroad. Let us try to understand quickly even before we are understood.

Father give us the strength to be resolute in our convictions to love in-spite of, even when our brother mean us harm; and give us the wisdom and strength to do what is best for our nations collectively and individually-even when we have to lovingly chastise our brother for the greater good-knowing full-well that the need of the whole out weight the need of a one or a few.

We thank you Father in advance for answering this prayer. We shall always be ever so careful to give you all the praise, honor, and glory for giving us the wisdom and knowledge to perform that which is good and right for all of our nations. It is in Jesus name that we pray-Amen.

A Leader's Prayer

Oh heavenly Father, the creator of heaven and earth, I give you all the honor, and all the praise, and all the glory. Thank you for all the blessings that you have bestowed upon me. Thank you for the wisdom and knowledge that you have given me—to be able to lead this group of people. Without you, I am not the best leader that I can be and have no sense to lead.

Thank you for giving me the wisdom and strength to hold me tongue during conversations with my enemies.

Thank you for holding my tongue during conversations with my friends.

Thank you for giving me the discernment to see so called friends who are really concealed enemies.

I pray right now Father that you will continue to allow me to dwell in your storehouse of wisdom, knowledge, and understanding, for I cannot lead these people without you. Give me a secret place that I might adjourn to when my feelings have been hurt, my emotions have been wounded, and my confidence is wavering.

Father, give me the strength to forgive those that brake the ranks and go astray; let me forgive those who have plotted ill for me even while standing next to me pretending to be on my side. Let my eyes remain on you while I walk this road called leadership.

Lord, keep my passions alive; my visions sure, and my purpose clear.

Thank you for rescuing me from me.

In Jesus name I pray,

Amen

The Road Of Leadership

It is the loneliest of roads of travel
Where the gravel the pavement and
the grassy lounge together
Mounds and pot holes lure and await the unsuspecting
And rob them of their bravery courage and confidence

THE ROAD OF LEADERSHIP

Where few friends travel
And most enemies are in hiding
The weary finds little or no rest
But the eyes fear to close

THE ROAD OF LEADERSHIP

There tongues lick and groom and lie
Where truth flees and promises never to return
Ears are but everywhere
And noses grow larger than life

THE ROAD OF LEADERSHIP

Where men regurgitate the truth
And digest lies
Where everybody is listening
And nobody hears

THE ROAD OF LEADERSHIP

Tis the road of honor where victory and defeat meet
Of brave men, of roaring lions, of
strong bears, of soaring eagles
Where the lamb becomes the wolf
And pride is worn upon the shoulder

THE ROAD OF LEADERSHIP

Where weakness is fatal
And loneliness is companion
But spoils are but spoils
It is the title that men thirst the position that separates

THE ROAD OF LEADERSHIP

That fails me to see me
That puffs me up bigger than me
That makes the poisons sweet like honey
That compels men to willingly leap to death for but title

THE ROAD OF LEADERSHIP

They stand in line to be slain of her
They deny their integrity for but a kiss from her
They abandon their families to walk with her
Their emotions are imprisoned by her

THE ROAD OF LEADERSHIP

The lonely road filled with misunderstandings
And unfulfilled dreams
Of mice and men
Of lions and weasels
Of fools and wise men
But still we race to the illusive darken road
Of leadership

HE THAT BOWS HIS KNEE TO GOD
CAN NEVER BE DEFEATED

YOUR DIS-POSITION
WILL DETERMINE YOUR POSITION

Just An Awful Mess

I am in just an awful mess
My nights and days be full of stress
All of this hurt confusion resting in my chest
Causing me to fail my daily test

JUST AN AWFUL MESS

I am just an awful fool
For therein I forsook my cool
And chose to leap back into life's constant duel
Carrying my emotions upon my heart like an old pack mule

JUST AN AWFUL MESS

Again I am disrespected
But I can't allow myself to be disrespected
So the best of me that's left must be collected
Before all of me is marred and affected
And the royalty in me go undetected

JUST AN AWFUL MESS

Here I go again arguing with me myself and I
Telling myself about myself while
trying desperately not to cry
Desiring something that even money cannot buy
Of love of passion of faithfulness of respect of no lie
Hoping of heaven's delight for loving on me before I die

JUST AN AWFUL MESS

But I must I must pick myself up
And empty the mess that's in my cup
For life's drink is not filled to one big gulp
But of ease through life like a gleeful happy pup

JUST AN AWFUL MESS

The lion in me must arrest the sheep in me
If I am to rise up to be
And protest the disrespect that I see
Thrown at me

JUST AN AWFUL MESS

Demand respect even at risk of being by myself
For if not all of me will flee until none of me is left
And my heart become deft
Stored in somebody's else abandoned shelf

JUST AN AWFUL MESS

I respect me
I force others to respect me
So they'll see the real me
Resting on me and getting rid of the awful mess within me

OTHERS WILL ONLY RESPECT YOU
TO THE DEGREE THAT YOU RESPECT YOURSELF

Proverbs

-The mouth simply echoes the abundance of the heart

-Most old men minds are a prison graveyard
Filled with shackled thoughts and
berried fresh consciousness

-When a man refuse to live
He is already dead and apt to die twice

-Organized religion
Is the new freedom for thoughtless cowardly men
Whose lives are filled with yester years and tomorrow's fears

-Never let your guards down
Around a man who cannot rule his woman

-He who does not lead at home
Is unworthy to lead abroad

-Increase your level of consciousness
And the world around you will change

Another Coon

Way back in the back deep woods of Mississippi, beyond the rolling hills and sleepy mountains; pass the moss riddled slumbering trees where slobbering greedy hogs run wild burrowing deep holes in the ground searching for roots to eat; way back pass the horizon of the glowing sun where billowing clouds roam slowly across a never ending blue sky, there rests a nameless town nestled in the valley of a nameless mountain; a town filled with people that time and the world had forgotten, where blacks live on one side of the forest and whites live on the other side.

Somewhere after the 1800s, but before the 1900s, this nameless town rested amidst the greenery and vibrant colors of lazy flowers and gleaming roses.

"Hoss get up now . . . . get up, to see if them hogs or them coons have bothered with the corn or them chickens?" Old man Nusbush yelled in the room of his slumbering son.

The sun was just peeking up over the mountains and easing through the leaves of the tall trees; chasing away the lingering shadows of the night while it silently slipped away.

"Hoss, you hear me boy? Get up. Them coons been up."

"Yea . . . . Yea . . . . Yea, I hear ya Pa." Hoss growled in his deep sleepy voice full of testosterone and last night's hard moonshine.

Hoss was a big ole young fellow-twenty-four years old; strong as an ox; tall, wide, muscular, and as hard as a young oak tree. He could drink the best of the old men under the table with his 6'8 inch frame. He'd stagger home after the rest of the men, young and old, had been slain and passed out from old man Luther's moon shine.

He rolled across the bed and hit the floor with a hard thump, still tangled in his sheets. Moonshine whispered loudly from his breath and echoed across the room.

"Ain't no coons out this morning." Hoss snarled to himself.

"What?" Mr. Nusbush snapped, turning his head sternly towards Hoss's room.

"Nothing Pa . . . . Nothing." Hoss slipped on his shirt, and stumbled hard while trying desperately to get on his trousers.

"That stuff ain't turned you lose yet?"

"Yea Pa." Hoss rubbed his hand through his bushy hair and scratched his scraggly beard as he walked pass old man Nusbush and out the door.

It felt good walking in the cool morning air. A light fog nestled low to the ground, as the cool morning dew dripped slowly from leaning slumbering leaves and splashed silently upon the mist filled grass. Hoss, now fully awaken, strode up to the small field of corn surrounded by a homemade wooden fence that never kept the hogs, or any other varmint that wanted a late night snack, out. And, sure enough, just like old man Nusbush thought, there were wild hogs helping themselves to a few stocks of corn.

Hoss, eased up closer, knelt down, nestled his shot gun in the clef of his shoulder, and rested his chin against the side of the gun as he took aim. He squeezed the trigger; a load of buck shot burst from the barrel searching for the would be target-leaving a trail of smoke easing from the barrel as a loud boom echoed through the morning silence of the sleepy forest.

A very large six foot long hog with eight inch sharp husk and a dark body with dirt riddled hair hanging all over, weighing well over four hundred pounds, hit the dewy ground hard as he let out his last squeal from a mouth full of corn, while his cohort corn thieves quickly ran off into the bushes squealing as they went.

"Got ya!" Hoss yelled out, waving his shot gun into air.

Briskly, he walked towards the Godzilla of a hog lying dead on the ground amidst a few stalks of corn.

"Hoss, is that you?" A soft woman's voice pierced the air, and stopped Hoss in his tracks.

"Huh, Rose, is that you?" Hoss said, turning towards the sound of the woman's voice.

"Yea, it's me."

"What you doing out here so early by yourself?"

"Mama sent me out here to get a piglet for dinner. We running a little short, and a piglet would be enough for us a few days; maybe even a week."

"Want me to help you?" Hoss asked.

"No, I already got one. It's laying over there in the brush," said Rose, pointing over Hoss's shoulder towards her waiting piglet dinner for her and her Mama.

"How'd you kill it? With that thing?" Hoss said pointing at the bow and sachet of arrows hanging around rose neck.

"Well, yeaaaa; this is good for the piglets; course it would do nothing for that hog monster you got laying over there. Side, how you gone get that thing home?"

"Um gone make an Indian stretcher, and pull him home."

"Only you Hoss . . . . Only you. That is too much meat-even for you and your family," said Rose looking down at the dead hog.

"No, it's my birthday party Saturday night. Um a roast this fellow-well most of him. You coming?"

"Yea, I heard. I'll be there," said Rose. "Look, I got to go take this piglet for Mama to prepare; she's waiting for me. I'll see you Saturday night birthday boy." Rose stepped up closer to Hoss, and gave him a big hug-squeezing him tightly.

Rose's hugs always made Hoss feel uncomfortable and a little embarrassed. Secretly, he had a crush on Rose, and felt like she liked him too, but didn't know how to show it.

Rose disappeared into the woods, dragging her piglet along side of her.

Hoss stared at Rose leaving, dragging the piglet along side of her, until he could see her no more. He made him an Indian stretcher, and rolled the huge hog onto it, and then dragged it home while thinking about how much fun he was going to have at his party Saturday night."

Old man Nusbush sat on the porch in his rocking chair, puffing on a long wooden homemade pipe of tobacco while talking to his friend Mr. Pine.

"Ya know Pine, we ought to go coon hunting today." Old man Nusbush said staring gleefully at Mr. Pine with a crooked grin on his face.

"Nawww, we don't coon hunt no more."

"Yea, we do. We just don't kill em no more; we just scare the hell outta them, and laugh while we watch them run off into the woods scared and hollering." Nusbush smiled broadly at Mr. Pine. Mr. Pine smiled back; reminiscing of how much fun they had had during the last coon hunt.

"Why, I saw a couple of coons early this morning strolling down by the river bank. I yelled at them, and boy, you should have seen them scattering off." Old man Nusbush laughed hard. "Come onnnnnn Pine; let's go scare some coons today."

"Ok .... Ok .... Ok, I ain't got nothing else to do, but we can't kill them; we are just going to scare them, and laugh hard while we watch them run into trees and stuff as they scramble away from us."

"Now that's what um talking about," said old man Nusbush as he got up to go get his shot gun.

Mr. Pine went to his wagon, and reached under his seat and got his old beat up weather worn shot gun. He leaned against the wagon and waited patiently for old man Nusbush to come out. He heard a bunch of rumbling and things being knocked over, and the clatter of glass.

"What you doing in there Nus?" Pine hollered out into the log built shack of a house.

"Here I come . . . . Here I come; just keep ya britches on. Them coons ain't going nowhere." He came out of the house with a sack full of buck-shots in his hand, and the shotgun tucked under his arm.

"Now we ain't gone shoot no coons are we? We just gone scare them, right?"

"Yea . . . Yea, come on, and quit worrying like an old woman-my god man."

They walked purposely into the thick of the forest and down several steep hills, and then up a few; looking for some coons that they could have fun with.
The screaming sun rested deep in the smooth sky; and clouds standing like puffs of smoke refused to give them any shade. Little forest critters scrambled to hide when they heard old man Nusbush and Pine coming-though they tried as they might to make little or no noise. Little Sparrows, blue birds, and Crows fluttered about amongst the tall trees, warning the other forest animals of the pending danger of approaching humans.

"I need to rest." Old man Nusbush said as he stopped and sat down upon the ground by an old leaning evergreen tree;

beads of sweat rolled down his cheeks and nestled under his chin.

"I thought you were ready to see some coons?"

"I am. Um just not ready to die trying to catch one."

Just then, they heard some rustling in the bushes about 50 meters away from them. Old man Nusbush pressed his finger upon Mr. Pine's mouth while he spoke-trying to get him to hush up in mid sentence.

Pine grabbed his hand, and slung it away from him.

Old man Nusbush pointed silently at the brush, and motioned for Pine to get ready. They spread upon their bellies on the ground, and aimed their shotguns at the rustling brush.

"Don't breath, just squeeze," whispered old man Nusbush to Pine.

Slowly, without a breath, they squeezed their triggers . . . .
BOOM!!!

"Mama." Hoss hollered out as he slid the huge dead hog into the front yard. "Mama."

"Coming Hoss, coming," said Mrs. Nusbush running to the door to see what excited Hoss was calling her for. "Good lord Hoss, where'd you get that thing from?"

"I killed it down in the corn field."

"Gosh, gone take us forever to clean that him."

"No it won't if all of us pitch in," said Hoss throwing the Indian stretcher to the ground.

"But, we got plenty of meat already."

"Not for my party Saturday."

"Yea, you right," said Mrs. Nusbush. "well, I guess we bess get started." She turned and went back into the house, rubbing her hands upon her already stained filled apron.

Hoss through the Indian stretcher with the lifeless hog on it hard to the ground, and then dragged the huge hog off of it, and turned it over onto its back. He grabbed his long knife, with a twelve inch blade, and started to slice the hog from its neck right down to its groin.

Old man Nusbush and Mr. Pine scrambled to their feet, giggling like two teenaged boys. They ran, as two old men full of age—wobbling all the way.

"Look at them run Pine . . . . Look at them run!" Nusbush hollered to Pine as they slid up to the brush where the coons had been.

Mr. Pine pulled the brush back to see what the coons had been doing behind the brush. He dropped his shot gun to the ground, and stumbled backwards.

"What? . . . . What? You look like you've seen a ghost." Old man Nusbush shouted at Pine.

Lowering his head into the palm of his hands, Pine pointed at the brush. Nusbush eased the brush back to see what was wrong with Pine. Splattered blood dripped from the shrubberies surrounding a little black boy. He laid there, with his smooth black skin and twisted locks of hair, lifeless, staring back at old man Nusbush. His young innocent brown eyes, still filled with would have been hope, would have been dreams, seemed to stare hard at Nusbush and ask why.

"Pull yourself together man. It's just a young coon."

"But he's a boy . . . . And we ain't supposed to be killing no coons nowadays. We could go to jail Nus," said Pine rising to his feet, shaking nervously.

"Whose gone tell we did it. We ain't going to jail for no coon," said Nusbush, taking the empty shells out of his shot gun, and tossing them aside. "Let's go; enough fun for today." He snapped angrily at Pine and walked hurriedly away.

"But."

"No buts, just keep your mouth shut; ya hear me Pine? Just keep your big mouth shut. We ain't going to jail for killing no coon."

They walked silently back to old man nusbush's house. The forest critters screamed their story as the trees swayed back and forth under the strength of the pending forthcoming judging wind that would soon fully arrive. Two black crows followed them overhead, flying from tree to tree, screaming of injustice as only crows can.

*   *   *

"Where's Pa, you say?" Hoss said, pulling the thick layers of fat away from the lean meat of the hog. He sliced and sliced until he had pulled all of the fat from the huge hog. He threw the last of the fat into the pile of the hog's insides that he had already pulled from him-guts and blood color the earth around Hoss and the hog.

"They went coon hunting."

Hoss stood up and stared hard at mama. "Why ain't they wait for me. I ain't been coon hunting in years; But the laws done changed now. You can't kill em. You just scare em."

"Yea, now I have to clean my own house and do my own cooking; just aint right. But, them coons stays on their side most of the time." Mrs. Nusbush stared off into the distance as she remembered the days when black folks were their slaves and their labor. "It's just crazy; darn crazy. Them coloreds was born to serve us, but them mixed up folks in Washington just messed thangs up for all of us."

"You right ma. Um a go see can I find them. Which way they go?"

Just then, Mr. Nusbush and Mr. Pine walked up in the yard. Old man Nusbush went straight into the house without parting a word to either Hoss or his wife.

"Pa . . . . Pa." Hoss hollered after him. "What's wrong with Pa," said Hoss, turning to Mr. Pine. "Y'all didn't see no coons?"

"No," snapped Mr. Pine, sliding his shotgun onto his wagon, and then jumping into the seat, and yelling at the mule to get going. "Getty up."

"Him and Pine must have gotten into it like they always do; specially when they didn't find no coons," said Mrs. Nusbush.

The night was hot and musty with no breeze stirring anywhere; even the crickets and the frogs of the night seem to scream and croak sluggishly. Waves of heat, judgmental heat, rested in the house, and bathed anybody that lingered there too long.

Hoss snored loudly, sleeping on the porch in a swing that creaked back and forth with every bit of his movement. Dressed in only his underwear, mosquitoes dined on his large hairy body, but it was of no consequence to him, for it was better than baking in the heat of the house.

Old man Nusbush tossed and turned back and forth, finding no rest or comfort for his conscious or his body. Streaks of pain ran across his chest and down his arm. His breaths were labored. He couldn't speak; couldn't even speak a word, or move a muscle for his wife that lay right next to him. Like some big hog had laid upon his chest, and refused to move, he was pinned to his lumpy old beaten worn mattress. Mr. Nusbush suffered, and suffered for what seemed like eternity all that night-finally falling off to sleep amidst the laboring pain shooting from his heart.

The sun had rose up over the still trees and shot beams of golden light upon the dew resting upon blades of sleepy grass. Humming birds flutter about seeking early morning breakfast, as the Morning Doves sang their daily ritualistic song to all that would listen.

Suddenly a loud scream echoed through the house and out the front door. It was Mrs. Nusbush screaming as she fell out of bed and onto the hard floor.

Hoss jumped, and fell out of the swing, and rushed to his feet, and then miss-stepped backwards off of the porch, and hit the ground like a falling oak.

Mrs. Nusbush burst through the front door looking wildly crazy, still screaming as she came.

"What's the matter Ma? What's the matter?" Hoss shouted. Mrs. Nusbush ran and stood behind Him.

"A coon! A coon was laying in the bed besides me.!"

"What?" Hoss stammered, walking towards the front door.

"Yea, a coon!" She shouted, peeking from behind Hoss and staring at the front door.

Mr. Nusbush eased to the door, rubbing his hand across his chest. He pushed the screen door opened and looked at his wife standing behind Hoss looking all wild eyed and crazy.

"What's wrong with you woman?" He said bewildered.

"I don't know what you doing here, but you got about two seconds to get out of here; don't um a fill you so full of buck shots till your mammie won't know you." Hoss said holding onto his mama's arm trying to protect her.

"Who you talking to boy?" Mr. Nusbush asked, walking out onto the porch.

"Hoss . . . . Hoss . . . . Do something," said Mrs. Nusbush.

"Woman! Get back in this house." Mr. Nusbush said, pointing his hand behind him towards the front door.

Hoss ran to get his shotgun leaning on a tree beside their old wood shed-Mrs. Nusbush followed closely behind him. He grabbed his shotgun and pointed it at Mr. Nusbush standing on the porch confused at it all.

"Now, you put that gun down Hoss; you hear me? Put that gun down boy."

"Damn coon; you got some nerve; I'll tell you that much, but not for long." Hoss pulled the double triggers back on the shotgun.

Mr. Nusbush quickly turned, for he could see in Hoss's eyes that he was going to fire; he turned and jumped through the screened door as a big doom echoed behind him and hot buck-shots chased behind him ever so closely.

"Boy, are you crazy?" Mr. Nusbush screamed out as he scrambled to get to his feet.

Hoss patted for his pockets, looking for more buck-shots, but forgot that he had no pants on. He ran onto the porch and slipped his pants on.

Mr. Nusbush heard Hoss's footsteps on the porch. He swirled around in utter confusion, wondering what to do, where to go.

Hoss reloaded the shotgun, and reassembled it with a loud click, and then eased the front door opened; it creaked loudly.

Old man Nusbush mind raced and swirled when he heard the creaking of the screened door. He knew that Hoss was on his way, and would gun him down without a second thought. He had no time to think of why his wife was afraid of him, or why Hoss was trying to shoot him; he just knew that he had to do something, and do something quick.

Hoss's foot steps eased slowly, one step over another, down the shadowy hall of the shack; Mrs. Nusbush closely behind-holding onto the back waste of Hoss's britches. He eased in, step by step, inch by inch. His breaths eased from his nostrils as beads of anxious sweat gathered upon his brow—expecting the unexpected.

Old man Nusbush's heart pound like a herd of galloping horses racing down the turn of the Kentucky derby race track. One thing that he was definitely sure of if nothing else-Hoss would shoot him without ever flinching. He saw Hoss's shadow lean into the doorway. He jumped with all of his might, and burst through the glass window and into the adjacent brush. He rolled down the hill, hearing buck-shots spray the bushes and branches of trees.

"How'd that coon get in here?" Hoss yelled out.

"I don't know; when I woke up, there he was laying beside me," said Mrs. Nusbush.

"Where is Pa?"

"Don't know what he did with him." Mrs. Nusbush wringed her hands, and walked back and forth, worrying about old man Nusbush's whereabouts.

Old man Nusbush ran and ran and ran until he had to stop. His heart felt like it would jump right out of his chest. He breath hard and couldn't get enough air. Nusbush looked around, trying to see what he could see; anything that would be helpful to him. He spotted the bank of the river that he had fish upon many times; he ran to it and kneel down and put his face into the water, and drank as much as he could.

Nusbush raised up, water dropping from his face back into the river. Suddenly, he jumped back when he saw his reflection in the water. He looked all around him to see if he could see anyone watching him, and then he eased back to the water and again looked at his reflection. He put his hands upon his forehead, and then ran them slowly down his face. He rubbed hard, thinking that he must have gotten some smoke or something on his face and hands.

"Dear lord, I look like a coon." He rubbed his hands upon his arms again as he dipped them in the water. "Um a coon; no wonder my wife was scared of me, and Hoss was trying to shoot me. Um a coon."

He tried hard to wrap his mind around what had happened to him last night. His face was black, his hair was curly, and his eyes went from blue to brown; yes, he was now black. Some way and some how, old man Nusbush had turn black over night. He had become the very people that he despised;

the people that he thought wasn't worth much; the people that he called coons; only worth killing are laughing at.

He wondered where the black folks lived; he didn't feel right, now to call black folks coons because now he was one. The sun had began to set over the distant grey mountains, and shadows eased in amongst the tall trees. Old man Nusbush still couldn't believe what has happened to him. He felt alone and isolated. He sat down and leaned against a tree as the heaviness of the day slowly crept upon his eyes while he gradually fell asleep, fighting hard to stay awake.

A large crowd had gathered at old man Nusbush's house; as word had gotten out that Nusbush had been taken during the night by a black man. They had dogs, and shotguns. Many of them acted like it was a regular party, for they drank their White Lightening moonshine whisky, and sent a few rounds of buck-shots into the night sky. They finally had an excuse to hunt black men again, men that they called coons.

"Y'all ready?" Hoss hollered into the crowd of white faces filled with moonshine, low self esteem, and anger. "Let's go get that coon that took my Pa."

They roared as loud as thunder as they followed Hoss and the herd of dogs on the trail of Nusbush.

Old man Nusbush was suddenly awakened by barking dogs and shining flash lights upon his face. He got up and ran, but it was no use; they were right on him. He leaped behind a bunch of bushes as a hoard of buck-shots trailed him in. They just fired and fired until their guns wouldn't shoot no more.

"Did we get him?" Somebody yelled out.

"Yea, we got that coon." Another yelled.

They all followed Hoss as he eased up to the bushes with his shotgun cocked, aimed, and ready to fire again-though it had no more buck-shots in the chamber. He eased the bushes back. Blood dripped from the leaning leaves. Old man Nusbush lay there filled with buckshot holes all over his body. They stared at him; some hollering in victory; some dancing about, and some just stared at the black body lying there in a pool of blood. Hoss stood there with a big grin on his face.

"Look." One of them shouted above the commotion. "Look y'all."

They all stopped and looked down at the black body. Slowly, right before their very eyes, old man Nusbush's body began to turn back to its original self; starting from his hair right down to his feet. His eyes turned back grey as they stared aimlessly back at Hoss and his excited peers. Their months fell open as they couldn't believe what had just happened before their very eyes. The black body disappeared and replaced it self with the white body of old man Nusbush. They had killed old man Nusbush-Hoss and his drunken followers. Fear leaped upon them like a hungry panther from the night sky.

Right today, in that little town deep in the forest of nowhere, there lives a group of people, black and white, who does not differentiate between color; who treats a man as a man without considering his color, for every time an issue of color or prejudice would come, the story of old man Nusbush would come up.

Hoss and his mama eventually lost their minds, and just slept away an early death-never forgiving himself for hunting down his own father and helping a lynch mob to kill him.

So, every time you should think of judging someone because of their skin color, just think of old man Nusbush; you just might some day be in their shoes.

LET US LIVE LIFE TO THE FULLEST
AND ENJOY OUR STUFF AND OUR THINGS
WASTE NOT ONE MOMENT
FOR DEATH WILL SOON COME
AND DISROBE US ALL

A STINGY MAN AND A GENEROUS MAN
WILL NEVER BE A RICH MAN

A Prayer For Dieing Mama

Mama, mama, oh mama
Why must you leave me so soon
And even if you left me in a thousand years
It would still be too soon

Oh heavenly Father; great God Jehovah, the creator and sustainer of everything—The One that breathed breathe into man, and made him a living soul. I give you all the honor, and all the glory, and all majesty, and all power.-for you are the only living God.
I thank you for the time that you have blessed me with mama. I thank you because I know that there be many children that did not have as much time with their mama as I have, and too, I thank you for allowing me to say goodbye.

Oh Father, I am constantly told that she is going to a better place, but I know not the place, and have never been there, nor know anyone that have gone there; and so, I do not know whether or not it is a better place, but I trust you! I trust that where ever the place of death is, you will keep your hands on my mama, for she trusts you so much-as I do as well.

Dear Lord, as you already know, I spend most of my time amidst grief and out-bursts of tears that won't soon go away or dry up; but still I thank you because her pain and suffering is coming to a close and ceasing.

You know Father that I am trying desperately to be strong, but the little boy in me (Mama's little boy) is frightened and scared, for I could always count on mama. She believed in me when nobody else did, or even when I had lost hope in my own self. She kept me on the right path.

Jehovah, I thank you for giving me such a mama, for I know that there be many children that are not so fortunate.

Please God, keep my mama-where ever she is going, whether to rest until you come for all of us that is still left here, or straight to heaven, keep her; for I know that You are a Keeper of souls.

And though now my tears sometimes run like rivers of water, I know that one of these days, they shall ease, and the little boy in me will calm down, and allow the man of me to press on and continue to serve you Jehovah until you decide too that it is my time to join the ranks of mama and all of them that will go before me.

Deer God, keep my heart safe, for it is now broken and hurting. Mama sleeps now most of the time, and I am told that her last week upon this side of life is fast approaching. Let not my faith waver, but give me the strength to keep believing and trusting you. I know that you got mama, as you have kept her all down through the years, as you are presently keeping her until she crosses over from life to death.

Thank you Great Jehovah for all of your goodness and mercy!!

AMEN.

Efil's Run

Efil's rocket ship zoomed through space with lightening speed-passed planets, passed stars, passed galaxies-forcing light years between him and those that gave him pursuit. He held the helm of his ship so hard until his hands and shoulders screamed with shooting pain, but he couldn't let go. His ship had to keep going, and he mustn't slow down, not for one moment, not a second; he had no time to spare.

General Htaed and his villainous army gave hot chase, and were determined not to let Fuji be their first condemned one to escape; no, they mustn't allow that. It would send the wrong message to other condemned future prisoners.

Efil's children, Evil and Syad sat wide eyed and strapped tightly to their seats; his wife, Mercy, also sat strapped down in her seat, hands clasped hard around the proton gun. Her fingers pressed gently upon the triggers, aiming behind them at anything that should follow them. She would do anything to help protect her family. She wished, with all of her might, that her sister, Hope, would soon show up-as she always did, often at the last minute; too, Mercy knew that the proton blaster wouldn't kill General Htaed. It would only slow him down, but that all she needed for right now-to give her family just a little more time together.

The ship started to tremble violently while leaving a trail of electro light smoke dust scattered across the black velvety star filled sky.

"I think this is it!" Efil yelled as loud as he could. "She coming apart."

"No she is not Brother-in-law." A woman's voice hollered out amidst the confusion. "You just hold her steady. I am going into this computer to see can I give this engine a little boost. Boy, that General Htaed gets on my last damn nerve."

"I knew you'd come big sis," said mercy.

"I always do don't I?" Hope said quickly while unscrewing the bolts on the computer panel, and at the very same time fighting to keep her balance.

Hope had disassembled her molecular structure, and rode a beam of light shooting through space, to get onto the ship.

"Ok, Ok, enough with the family reunion," said Efil to the top of his lungs. "Hope, can I get some extra juice to this engine? My GPS is showing that General Htaed is just a few light clicks away, and will be upon us in less than fifteen minutes if we don't come up with some more energy for my ship."

"Just don't get your shorts in a ward Brother-in-law; I got this. We're about to make the General eat some cosmic dust." She slammed into the computer's modular a neutron electro booster.

Suddenly, the ship burst forth faster than the speed of light, and warped into another distant galaxy passed a mammoth black hole.

"Was that a Neutron Elec?" Efil shouted.

"Yea, and you can thank me later for saving your butt once again," said hope playfully.

"Well, one thing about you, you'll always save us, if you don't kill us first."

"Yea . . . . Yea." Hope muttered back at Efil while stepping upon a little spider. "Damn, I hate spiders."

"Thanks Sis," said Mercy, jumping from behind the proton gun, and giving Hope a big hug.

The children, Evil and Syad-a boy and a girl, jumped from their seats and ran past Efil into the waiting arms of their aunt-Hope.

"Well, don't thank daddy; I just only save your lives every now and then." He said sarcastically, peering over at the children jumping into Hope's arms.

Mercy ran up to Efil, and fell into his arms. "You're always my hero." She said, holding him tightly.

*   *   *

General Htaed slammed his cup of hot gin and coffee against the bronze brazen wall of his ship's lavish control room. His soldiers stirred about, trying to act as though they didn't notice the General's out burst of anger. He stirred about, pacing the floor back and forth. He gracefully rubbed his long slender fingers through his beard, deeply pondering his next move to capture Efil's and his crew.

He stopped and stared down hard at the GPS system; hoping to find a glimpse or any sign of Efil's whereabouts. He slammed his fist into the face of the GPS system-smashing it into a thousand pieces; again, his men tried to act as though nothing had happened. They were used to his fits of anger. Father Time had not simmered him at all, though he was almost as old as Father Time himself.

"How is it that this . . . . this . . . . this piece of crap of a man can evade me for so long. I've captured everybody except his monkey butt," argued General Htaed. "None has escaped me . . . . None . . . . No not one."

"Sir, I got them," said one of his lieutenants excitedly.

"Where?" General Htaed quickly walked over to him.

"They are somewhere in quadroon six."

"Is that right?" The general said easily, almost without parting his lips. Suddenly, he back slapped the Lieutenant with the back of his hand. "Do you know how big Quadroon six is? We could be looking there for years, and never find them." He shouted as loud as he could.

The lieutenant scrambled to his feet, and stood at attention; a few drops of blood trickled from his nose.

"Will someone come and fix this GPS please?" The general growled in discuss.

The control room rumbled into action with the soldiers running about like bees in a hive.

General Thaed realized how so very close this time he had come to capturing Efil—which meant, to him, that Efil was slipping. He thought to himself that sooner or later, he would catch him as he had eventually captured all of his other out of control villains of order.

"Will somebody bring me a drink?" He snapped. "And, make sure it is piping hot."

Several of them jumped at the sound of his orders. They knew that he only drank hot gin and hot coffee-a cup filled half full of gin and half full of coffee. He drank this all day; one after another. Most very rarely saw him eating anything-just always sipping on a cup of hot gin and coffee.

He studied the huge cosmic map, hologram on the wall. General Thaed stared and rubbed his hand slowly through the hologram.

"Where are you? You're out there somewhere." He mumbled to himself. Chasing Efil was now his passion.

General Thaed's pursuit of Efil was the talk of the universe. From one quadroon to another; from one galaxy to the other, everyone knew of the drama of Efil and General Thaed. Most praised Efil for accomplishing something that no one else had done-many were afraid to even attempt to evade the General, so Efil was their hero. Others despised him, for they felt that he was disrupting the natural flow of the universe. The General was the law that governed the course of everything. They thought that Efil's defiance threw the whole universe out of order, for everything and everybody had to surrender to General Thaed sooner or later; but they were equally afraid of both, General Thaed and Efil.

Quadroon six was filled with several planets, black holes, and moons. Efil knew that, which is why he chose quadroon six.

He had avoided being captured by General Thaed mostly by time hopping, but now, his Time Module had been blown up, and he hadn't had time to repair it.

He had decided to hide out in quadroon six to buy enough time to fix the Time Module so he could hop to earth, and hang out awhile. He knew that General Thaed hated earth, and would be most reluctant about following him there.

The ship was floating about, still smoking and tingling with electrical sparks here and there. Besides the Time Module, the Molecular Transporter, which gave them the ability to beam down to surface atmosphere, was also damaged.

Efil raced about conveying the damage to his ship. He argued to himself about evil General Thaed refusing to give up chasing him.

Three moons dominated the dark endless sky of quadroon six. A glowing ship, along with shooting comets zipped across the starry sky every now and then. Efil worked hard and steady, trying to repair the damaged age riddled ship, while the rest tried their very best to reorganize the clutter everywhere. He knew that he needed another ship; it's just so much pitch and patching that one could do to an old ship.

"I sure could use your brother Grace right about now," said Efil to Hope while tinkering with a few gadgets.

"He's on his way. I've already summoned him along with my younger sister, Love; she is a big help when you don't know what to do when your back is up against a wall."
"And you think that my back is up against a wall-huh?" Efil said, stopping and turning to look at her.

"Duhhhh . . . . Yea." Hope said, pointing at all the cluttering and smoking broken gadgets around them.

"And she is going to counsel how to get through this?"

"Yea, cause she'll help you gain peace during your time of trouble," said Hope. "And, looks like to me, you sure could use a little bit of peace right about now."

"Yea . . . . Yea . . ." He turned, and started back to working on his broken ship.

"We got his location General." One of the young engineers said, running up to the General.

"You'd better be right."

"The computer picked up the molecular fumes of dust seeping from Efil's ship. It leaves a trail eons long behind him."

"Even if he Time Hops?" General Thaed snapped, looking menacingly at the young soldier.

"Yes sir, even if he Time Hop; he still leaves a trail through the vortex. It's like his ship is slowing bleeding, and leaving a trail of blood behind it-where ever it goes, and long after it has passed.

"Great. Set a course for quadroon six, and follow the trail of dust." He whipped out his commands at soldiers sitting at the controls of his ship. "Prepare the Neutron lasers to fire on my command."

Efil and his family, his wife Mercy, his children Evil and Syad sat around the table eating with their visiting relatives-Hope and Grace, and their sister Love had only moments ago arrived.

They sat talking about how the cosmic universe had changed, and how the inhabitants in each galaxy had become so disconnected.

"Looks like we're going to have to get some place and settle down," said Efil.

"How we gone do that with that mean man following us?" His little girl, Evil interjected.

"Don't know sweetie."

"But, we're going to be alright whatever daddy decides." Mercy said, rubbing her hand through the ebony locks of Evil's hair.

"And we're going to make sure of that," said Hope, holding Grace and love's hand.

"Well, I got to get back going. This ship isn't going to fix . . . ."

Suddenly, a blast from a neutron cannon smashed upon the ship, and send all of them sailing in the air. Efil scrambled to his feet, rushing his family to their feet.

"Get in the pod." He shouted.

"But there is only one. How we gone do that, and it's not working well," said Mercy, as she and the other's ran and crammed into the Time Hopper pod.

"We have no choice. We cannot take another direct hit from that cannon. If we die, we shall all die trying to live.
Evil slammed the door shut on the Time Hopper pod. They were crammed in, and could barely move. He pushed the red button on the Hopper. Just as their body's molecular structure was in the midst of changing, another neutron blast it the ship-breaking it into a million pieces.

"Any survivors?" General Thaed whipped anxiously.

"None." A soldiers replied instantly.

"Body count." He said.

There was silence, for the young soldier knew that the General wouldn't want to hear his reply.

"Body count." The General snapped again.

"Er . . . . Ah . . . . None sir."

"Damn!!" He swung his fist into the air. "They got away again . . . They got away. But, I'll spend my every day chasing Efil; and one of these days I shall catch up to him . . . . Sooner or later, I shall catch up to him.

Efil, Mercy, Evil, Syad, Hope, Grace, and Love fell to the earth from the last of the Time Hopper's power. The sun rested beyond grey mountains off in the distance, while white billowing clouds eased across the sky.

They helped each other up. "Where are we?" Mercy said, looking at Efil.

"Earth, I always set the Time Hopper for earth, just in case; for it is the only place that General Thaed is apprehensive about coming too."

Efil and his family spent most of their time replenishing earth, and taking care of the different animals that roamed the planet. Every now and then, they would stare off into the vast night sky and see the twinkling stars, and remember when they once flew amongst them, or Time Hopped from one galaxy to another; but deep in the back of their mind, far into their subconscious, they always wondered when would General Thaed catch up to them-they knew that he would one day.

Now, General Thaed spends all of his days chasing and destroying anything that reminds him of Efil, while he passionately pursues Efil's where about.

Efil had decided that when he died, he would die upon earth. He helped the flowers to bloom, trees to grow, and helped keep peace between the animals and man. But, he knew, deep within his heart, that one day General Thaed would definitely catch up to him, but until then, he would spend the rest of his time LIVING.

THE MOST DIFFICULT THING FOR A PARENT
TO EXPERIENCE
IS TO HAVE TO BURY THEIR CHILD

THE MOST DIFFICULT THING FOR A SON
TO EXPERIENCE
IS TO HAVE TO BURY HIS MOTHER

My Mama's Death Bed

I sit by mama's bed filled with fears
Trying desperately to hold back my painful tears
While others sit back intoxicated by a few beers
My painful sobs I hope no one hears

Death eases upon mama's bed taking a little of her every day
I sit there praying and not knowing fully what to say
The preacher tells us that we should be happy and gay
That mama's on her way
Off of her sick bed to a better place to lay

Her many whippings kept me out of
prison and the graveyard
Simply refusing to let her son grow up to be too hard
Watching me become a man was her greatest reward
Not allowing some astrological sign to
determine my fate in a card

Dear mama what am I to do when you are gone
No longer able to call you every day at home
Never can I repay you for the years of love shown
That guided me to become fully grown

I watch them give you that morphine
Trying to ease the horrid pain that you've never seen
Making you become little and lean
I hope at least you're having a few sweet dreams

I think about when I was a little boy
You buying me every little toy
Bringing your little boy mounds of joy

Akeam Simmons

I pray that God helps me get through
For already I am missing you
And the wonderful things that you use to do
Turning my dark skies blue

It is so painful that you are about to leave me
But I am happy for from that ailing body you'll be free
To take a bite from heaven's living tree
And live in places that we could never see

Money

MONEY IS THE CORE OF ALL EVIL
IT SEPERATES FAMILIES
AND TURNS BROTTHERS AGAINST BROTHERS
FATHERS AGAINST SONS
IT IS THE LIGHTED THREAD THAT
CONNECTS THE WORLD
AND AT THE VERY SAME TIME
IT IS THE DARKENED THREAD THAT
DISCONNECTS THE WORLD
WOMEN MARRY MEN THAT
THEY DON'T LOVE
FOR MONEY
AND SELL THEIR
MOST PRECIOUS GIFT
FOR MONEY
MEN BETRAY THEIR MOST TRUSTED FRIEND
FOR MONEY
STILL IT IS COVETED BY ALL MEN
AND CHERISHED BY ALL WOMEN
IT IS IMPOSIBLE TO LIVE WITHOUT IT
AND PAINFUL TO LIVE WITH IT
IT PAYS FOR SOME MEN'S FREEDOM
AND PUTS MANY A WOMEN IN THEIR CHOSEN
PRISONS

By Myself

I lean over you upon your dying bed
My tears dropping upon your death riddled face
You lie expressionless as death steals your last bits of life
The other part of me
The best part of me eases into the unknown oblivion
Unto that place that no traveler returns from

I hurt
I thirst to hold you one last time
To scream out of how much I love you
How much I appreciate you
And am thankful for the priceless time you invested in me

Though I saw death easing into your room months ago
I never considered that you would soon leave me
For you were always supposed to be with me
Just thought that you would always be here

You are gone
Now those that refused to come visit you while you lingered
Pretend to weep of sorrow
Would that I could whip all of them to appease my flesh
But too I know it is not what you would wish of me

I hold your limp hand in my own hand
Feeling it grow cold as life flees from you
I whisper things in your ear
Knowing full well that my voice to you
Have grown silent and deaf
But I whisper in your ear anyway
Hoping that God would allow you to hear me this last time

Use to be you and I against the world
Now I stand alone
Amongst haters pretenders and perpetrators
Telling me with tongues of poison
How much they care
My condolences

How many times you denied yourself for me
How many times you took food from your plate
To put on mine
How many times during winter
You took your only coat off to put on me
So I would be warm while you were cold

Now I stand by myself
Holding a limp lifeless body
That says you are no longer home

By myself to fight the ones that you use to fight for me
By myself to walk in your memories
By myself to weep upon my own shoulders
And dry my own tears

By myself to fight the fight of faith
That you fought up till your last breath
By myself to force myself to keep on loving
In-spite of my hurt and pain

By myself to miss you more and more each passing day
By myself to forge ahead without you in my life
But a part of you is always with me deep inside of me

247

Akeam Simmons

By myself fighting to keep you alive inside of me
Making sure that my babies don't ever forget you

I know full well that some day
I shall be forced to walk down this same path called death
As so many of your fore—parents did before you
But I refuse to believe that I will be by myself
For if possible you shall walk with me
As I cross over
Or be there waiting and welcoming me to my new home
Where I won't be BY MYSELF NO MORE

WASTE NOT ONE MOMENT
TO CHERISH MAMA
FOR WHEN HER HEAD IS COLD
YOU SHALL WISH THAT YOU HAD
FOR LYING IN HER STATE OF DEATH
SHE CANNOT SMELL THE
FLOWERS THAT YOU BRING
NOR FEEL YOUR TEAR DROPS UPON HER FACE
OR APPRECIATE ALL THE MONEY
THAT YOU PUT IN THE GROUND FOR HER
NO
GIVE HER FLOWERS NOW
WEEP FOR HER NOW
THAT SHE MIGHT SEE YOUR TEARS
SPEND YOUR MONEY UPON HER NOW
THAT SHE MIGHT APPRECIATE
WHAT YOU HAVE
SPENT UPON HER

A Blade For The Dying

Beams of golden sunlight bathed the sky and rested heavily upon David's brow. Drops of sweat rolled and zig zagged quickly down his cheeks and splashed violently upon his chest. His breaths were short and shallow; his eyes rolled upon his bushy wild brow and rested at the edge while staring into nothing beyond his soon to be dead enemies.

His blade, soaked in blood, hollered and screamed as he slowly dragged it over the hot smoking parched dry desert ground; it tore a deep line in the dirt as it followed behind him; its handle resting easily in the palm of David's hand. He shifted his grip; readying himself to attack or be attacked.

David had slain thousands of others during his quest to find these two; the two warriors that had taken so much from him. They had slain many of his loved ones-his mother, his father, many of his friends, and just recently, his son. No, they could not escape this time; even if it meant him losing his own life. He had to avenge his loved ones for all that these two heartless warriors had taken from them.

They stood there, two fearless warriors, who had fought against and won against many a brave and gallant men. Their names were Death and Sickness. They stood there in the beaming grimacing sun, waiting for David's attack. They had met many times before; blades clashing like thunder and lightening, but only wounding one another's pride; for only a few escaped Death and Sickness attack, but none had survived an attack by David-no, not one.

He was wounded; blood oozed and eased down his side, but he was not deterred. The honor of his kinsmen rested this day upon his shoulders, upon his blade, and he had no intentions of letting them down. Pain raced from his wounds and ran sharply across his abdomen.

David could tell though, that he had wounded both Death and Sickness, as they stood there trying to hold their warrior defensive stance. He sensed their concern and pain, for it etched and screamed from their hollowed stares.

Slowly he eased his blade up from the dust riddled simmering ground, and prepared to attack.

Death and Sickness shifted their stance and prepared for David's
Attack. Somebody had to die today; it was time for one of them, or all of them to pay life's piper.

He leaped high, his sharp blood bathed blade sliced through the smothering hot air, racing towards its target. The clanging of blade upon blade filled the silence, as nature itself had paused to witness the outcome of this long overdue battle that would end this day.

The battle raged on and on until soon the sun got tired and eased beyond the tall trees and rested itself in the on coming shadows of night. The night's critters began to dance from the music made from the endless sounds of the clashing blades-yet the battle raged on; day in and day out. If you listen carefully in the night, you can still hear Davids's blade clashing upon Death and Sickness blades, and every now and then a faint grumble here and there.

251

Miss Mable's Lemonade

Everybody loved Miss Mable's lemonade; so cold, so refreshing, so tasty was it that the whole community raved about how good Miss Mable's lemonade was. The town's dignitaries and even the town drunks came in the evenings to get some of Miss Mable's lemonade to mix with their drinks of the evening.

She picked her lemons fresh from her own lemon tree in her back yard. Miss Mable gave some of the children in the community a dime to come over and toss, beat, and play with the lemons to soften them up; for she said, 'they ain't ready to be lemonade when they comes fresh off the tree,' and besides, the children playing with the lemons filled them with love so that when she cut them opened, the bitter juice would already be mixed with sweet children's love.

Miss Mable's lemonade, oh how good it was resting upon cubes of ice. She sold it a glass for only a dime, for she knew that if they tasted one glass of her lemonade, they were sure to get at least another; sometimes, on a hot day, men would sit and drink five glasses of Mable's lemonade.

The day was hot and musty. The sun beamed down hard upon the tin roofs of Mable's community. Waves of heat lingered upon the roads and around the houses. It was even hot under the trees, in the shade, and you need not mention how hot it is in the house, where Mable had several fans blowing all the time.

On this hot day, Mable had a visitor; an unpleasant visitor, one that she could certainly do without. It was Mr. Abraham, the owner of Liberty National Bank down town. He sat on Mable's old beaten couch, lumpy from holding her ten children and a many of grand children; and though her furniture was old, she still kept her house clean and tidy. Her couch and chairs were covered with clean fresh towels and sheets; and fresh flowers donned her tables, while the aroma of budding roses filled the air in the rooms of her house.

Though Mable sold much Lemonade, it was not enough to pay the house note every month and keep food on her table for her grand children, and her children that stopped by every Sunday after church for a big Sunday dinner—not to mention that Pastor Thomas and his wife would often stop by too. Nobody made collared green and fried chicken like Miss Mable; and her corn bread cooked on top of the stove, in her favorite iron skillet, was simply to die for. Every Sunday Miss Mable had a house full after church. She loved cooking and sharing what she had cooked.

She made everybody in the neighborhood happy, but nobody knew the struggles that Miss Mable was going through; nobody knew that she was about to lose her house. She was a very private old lady and full of pride.

"Now Mable, I've worked with you long as I can," said Mr. Abraham, wiping the sweat from his brow. "You know that. I just can't give you any more time . . . . I just cant."

"But I needs more time Mr. Abraham; I needs more time," said Mable, wringing her hands as she spoke. "You knows that I'll give it to you. It's just hard for an old widow lady like me. Me husband, Ben and me, was faithful to you, and paid you on time; but when he died, well, it's just been hard."

"I do understand Mable, but I am a business man; so either you have the money by next Wednesday, or I am going to have to repossess this property."

"Mr. Abraham, I knows why you wants my land." Mable said with hints of anger in her voice.
"And why is that Mable?" Mr. Abraham said condescendingly while staring at Mable over his glasses.

"Cause you wants to build that mall out here, and you needs my land to do it, but you don't want to pay me for this land that me and Ben worked so hard for."

Mr. Abraham put on a fake smile, and rubbed his hand through his straggly beard. "Well, think what you want to think Mable; I am a business man. Remember, by Wednesday Mable . . . . by Wednesday." He started to gather all of his papers together as he prepared to leave.

"I understand Mr. Abraham; well, at least have a glass of my good ole cold lemonade to refresh you before you go; god it's so hot."

Mable knew that it was hot; hot inside and outside. Mr. Abraham sat there sweating like a roasting pig. He kelp wiping his face as rolling sweat ran down his face. She refused to turn on a fan for him because she needed him to get too hot; she needed for him to need a cold glass of her lemonade.

"Mr. Abraham, let me go in the kitchen and get you a cold glass of that icy lemonade that I gots in my frigerator," said Mable as she got up, without waiting for him to answer, and started walking towards the kitchen.

"Yea, that would be nice Mable." He said. "You know that this is just business, don't you." Mr. Abraham yelled after her into the kitchen.

"Yea, just business; we all do what we have to do to survive, don't we?" She yelled back.

After a little while in the kitchen, with glass clanging and the sound of ice banging against the glass, Mable emerged from the kitchen with a big glass of ice cold lemonade. She carefully handed it to Mr. Abraham.

He drank it quickly without ever lowering the glass for air. The ice sang out as he finished the last of the lemonade and exhaled loudly.

"You look like you need another glass Mr. Abraham." She said, taking his glass and heading back off to the kitchen. "Yea, I understand Mr. Abraham. We all do what we have to do to survive; don't we." Mable yelled back into the living room.

"Yea . . . Yea, Mable; nothing personal. It's just business." He quickly downed the second glass of Mable lemonade, then rose to his feet.

"It's a shame what happened to Mr. Johnson last year; ain't it," said Miss Mable as she took the glass from Mr. Abraham's hand. "He was fixing to come repossess my stove. God knows I needs my stove; they say he just died in his sleep."

"Yes, it was unfortunate, but all of us have got to die sooner or later Mable."

"And what about old man Jones that owned the general store? You know he was fixing to come get my bedroom furniture. His wife says that it was a heart attack. Sweet lady; she told me not to worry about the furniture."

"Well, I take good care of myself, and I eat right."

"Let me get you another glass of this cold lemonade before you go back out in that heat." She ran back off into the kitchen before he could ever answer her, and was back, in a flash, with another big glass of ice cold lemonade. Carefully, she handed it to him-not wanting to spill a drop.

"Thank you Mable; now this is truly my last glass. I must be going." Quickly, he drank the lemonade without stopping for a breath."

He put his hat on, tucked his briefcase under his arm, and then walked out Mable's front door with a crooked smile upon his face.

"Remember, Wednesday Mable . . . Wednesday."

Mable just mumbled to herself, and then turned to go into the kitchen to clean up the mess that she had made while hurriedly preparing Mr. Abraham's special lemonade.

Miss Mable sat, in a squeaking rocking chair, on her porch Wednesday morning while her cat lay lazily upon her lap. She rubbed the cat's back and hummed a soft tune to herself.

The sun had just eased up over the old community (a community long years ago that use to be filled with slaves), and shot beams of golden sunlight over the roof tops and along side of the houses, chasing away the lingering sleepy morning dew.

She loved this time of morning. She would always say that this was God's time of day; it was when he was waking up mother earth and tucking in all of his night critters and waking up those that had slept all night.

Miss. Mable just hummed and prayed while the rocking chair kept squeaking a melody of its own.

"Miss. Mable . . . . Miss. Mable!" An excited voice from a young girl filled the air as she ran up to Miss. Mable's porch.

Startled, Miss. Mable, sat up in her rocking chair; the cat leaped to the floor.

"Miss. Mable . . . . Miss. Mable, have you heard the news?"

"What news child? What news?"

"About Mr. Abraham," said the young, trying to catch her breath.

"What about him Lisa? Talk child, talk."

"He left last night."

"Left?" Mable asked, rising to her feet.

"He gone to the other side. They says that he died last night in his sleep."

Miss. Mable reached down and grabbed her cat, sat back down in her rocking chair, and began rocking again and humming her favorite tune-Amazing Grace.

"Well?" The young girl said, looking deeply into Miss Mable's eyes.

"Well what child?"

"Well, how you feel about that? Everybody knew Mr. Abraham.

"Yea, and most of us over here owes Mr. Abraham," said Miss. Mable staring hard back at the confused young girl. "Guess he done cheated his last customer and repossess his last house."
"Guess so."

"Guess you better gone and tell others in the community about Mr. Abraham; gone make a lot of folks happy, and breathe a breath of fresh air; at least for a little while."

The young girl ran off into the morning air as birds donned the sky singing songs as they went.

"The Lord show is good," said Miss. Mable leaning back in her rocking chair. "Thank God for good ole Lemonade."

The Other Me

Oh whoa is me
Oh whoa is me
For I have yet to only glance to see
The folly that rests in me
With even the multitude of years it refused to flee
And let me be

Oh whoa is me
For there be another side of me
The dark side that others fail to see
Resting waiting in me
For opportunity to be
The beast the beast the other side of me

The hell raiser
The trail blazer
I be but another wealth chaser
Whose eyes become but burning lasers
That musters the beast in me to become crazier

The beast plucks the eye of my mind out of mental socket
It be difficult to fly to other horizons upon my mental rocket
Forcing my psychological docket
To be filled with disillusioned things to block it

But I force myself to be alright
For mama raised me to fight
And fight with all my might
To never allow myself to truly lose sight
Of the real things of life that would make me right

The other me
The other of which you cannot see
Fights with me constantly
To gain control of my faculty

Constantly I sigh
For my greatest fight is with me myself and I
Would that the other me would die
But would I be bidding the real me goodbye
And live a lie
Soon becoming only half a soul with no happiness nigh

The other me is as real as can be
He you just cannot see
But he is a great part of me
Sometimes standing for me when I can't face reality
And helping me not to be just another of life's casualty

So be careful how you treat me
For you know not when it is the other me
He is not as gentle or courteous as me
But still he is me
The other me

HAPPY IS A WOMAN
TO HAVE AN OLD WORKING MAN
THAN
A SORRY YOUNG MAN
FOR HE WILL ONLY ASPIRE TO BE
WHAT SHE AFFORDS HIM TO BE
NO MORE

THERE BE FEW THINGS WORSE
THAN A SORRY YOUNG MAN
WHOSE PLEASURE IS REST
AND WHOSE TIME IS SPENT UPON DREAMING
OF THE WEATH OF OTHERS

NEVER THROW A WOUNDED SHEPHERD
TO GRACING SHEEP
FOR IN DOING SO
YOU WOUND ALL SHEPHERDS

WE ARE ALL BUT EARTHEN VESSELS
INDIVIDUAL PIECES OF CLAY
COVERED WITH CRACKS AND HOLES
WE DECEIVE OURSELVES
WHEN WE TRY TO BE IRON
OR EVEN WORSE STEEL
GOD IS THE POTTER
THAT KEEPS THE EARTHEN CLAY
THAT IS COVERED WITH CRACKS AND HOLES

Great Is My God

Most don't understand the degree of my happiness
Or how much my God has blessed
So when storms come my way I am not stressed
Cause I know that it is only my test

He keeps me close even upon his breast
And gives his love fresh in my chest
Strengthening me to walk in His righteousness
Holding me up like His proud crest

My sins to him I confess
Then he gives me a message for my mess
And pours down upon me His peace and rest
That I might walk in His faithfulness

And though I might fall sometimes and regress
He doesn't love me any less
Or hold me hostage in my own failing recess
For my soul he still possess

For my good he doesn't always say yes
Because yes sometimes will hinder my divine progress
And ultimately cause me too much stress
To realize the blessing that I already possess

Ignoring my haters and life's pest
I hurry on filled with God's zest
Step by step day by day moving onward upward in progress
Being enriched with His holiness

I am not good enough even at my best
To stand up to life's constant test
Still He allows me to abide in his spiritual nest
While keeping me covered with His holy dress

I am not some ornament sitting upon the master's desk
For other celestial persons to look at and guess
Just as far as East is from West
I am separated from my sins and
filled with His righteousness

My body is but an earthen vest
That the master can show some of his creative best
So I am not quick to protest
When he choose to put me to the test

Every day I do confess
Of His goodness and righteousness
And thank Him for strengthening me to walk in holiness
Until my day is done and He calls me to His rest

A Bleeding Heart

Laura sat in bed with her chin resting upon her knees while watching her husband, Lesley, get dress for work. It was four in the morning, and it seemed as though they had just shut their eyes a few moments ago. Lesley had gotten home from his other job last night around 11; now, here he was getting ready to go to his third job.

Laura loved her husband with all of her heart. She hated to see Lesley work so hard and stay gone most of the time, but she knew that they had bills to be paid, and she loved shopping; too, guilt laid upon her breast like a ton of bricks. She sat there with a broken heart-grieving for her husband. 'How could any man be so dumb and stupid, and yet so utterly loving at the same time.' She asked herself over and over again while watching him get dressed.

"Why can't you just quit one of these jobs Les?" Laura pleaded with her husband. "We'll get by."

"Okay, you decide which goes back; the Mercedes, the Cadillac, or the BMW, or all of them cause you know that if I lose any one of my jobs, we can't afford those cars; not to mention your spending habits," said Lesley, straightening his tie as he looked into the mirror. "This life style cost. You know that Laura."

"Yea, I know, but I miss you so much. I just thought that we could cut back on some things so that we wouldn't need that much money."

"Cut back on what?" Lesley snapped at her.

"I don't know. I am just so lonely here most of the time. I need you here." She laid back and berried her head in the fluffy pillow.

"You think that I don't want to be here . . . . Huh?" He asked her, walking up to the bed and sitting down beside her. He gently, caringly ran his hand through her locks of curly hair as he spoke ever so softly to her. "Things are not going to be this way always honey. I just got to get us out of this financial mess that we've made. Just give me another year."

"A year!" She screamed and withdrew from his touch.

"Well, I got to go; we'll talk about this later." Lesley grabbed his briefcase and walked out of the room, and out of the house.

Laura lay there with tears streaking down her face. She hated what she had become. It was hard to even look at herself in the mirror, but it was getting easier and easier every day to accept the life style that she was secretly living. She had become the lady that she and her girlfriends would gossip about over their lunch martini at the mall after shopping and spending their husband's money.

She picked herself up off of the bed and staggered into the shower, and showered long and hard, as if trying to wash something off that refused to come off. She eased into her favorite most provocative night gown, and turned on some soft music, music that one could barely here. Her perfume ravaged her body and leaped into the air and spread profusely throughout the room. She went into the kitchen and poured herself a glass of wine, and then sat upon the love chair that she and Lesley never used.

Three faint taps whispered from the front door. Laura took another big gulp of wine from her glass; stood up and looked down at herself as she tugged softly at her gown. She headed for the door while primping her hair as she went. Finally reaching the front door, she paused for a moment, took a deep breath, and then slowly opened the door.

Standing on the other side of the threshold was Moseby; a young man fifteen years younger than she. He stood there with all of his robust masculinity pouring from him and immediately engulfing her-all of her. He simply took her breath away. Laura hated what she had become, but she love the way Moseby made her feel. She was helpless and weak with him; and though she wanted to stop and resume the life of a faithful wife, she couldn't; her heated yearning body wouldn't let her.

Moseby made her feel alive again; he quickened every part of her body, even the parts that she had forgotten and thought was dead; he made her thirst again for life and liveliness. His very touch made her limber, weak, and overflowed with passions delight.

"Hey you." He said barely above a whisper.

A smile raced across Laura's face; her heart raced as if it would simply jump out of her chest at any moment.

"Hey, she whispered back."

"Well, can I come in."

"Oh, um sorry; come on in," she said while motioning for him to enter.

Moseby crossed the threshing. She slowly eased the door shut and locked it. He wrapped his arms around her and drew her in close to him. She whimpered; her body went weak as she laid her head upon his chest. Her perfume mingled with his cologne created an aphrodisiac that made both of them helpless to even think about resisting the moment. Right then, the world stopped; nothing else matter-not time, or place, or what wondering neighbors eyes might see, or their minds might imagine. She was hooked, willingly hooked; and it felt good. Feeling a man's touch in the early morning while her hormones were raging and searching, was more than she could bare.

After Moseby had eased from the house, Laura lay there, amidst the soft music, entangled in her sheets. A smile slipped across her face as she reflected upon wrestling passionately with Moseby a few moments ago. But then, shame and degradation leaped upon her like a lioness upon her prey. She unwrapped herself of the sheets, and ran into the shower. She promised herself, as usual, that it would never happen again, but she knew deep within her subconscious mind, that she was hooked like a helpless fish wrestling upon a fishermen's hook. She exhaled and scrubbed hard with the soap while the water raced down her side.

It was four in the morning, and Lesley was standing in front of the mirror getting dress. Laura lay in bed quietly with her head resting on her arm.

"What? Cat got your tongue this morning?" Lesley said as her tied the last of his tie.

Laura didn't respond; she just lay there amidst her own private thoughts as tears swelled in her eyes.

"Don't worry. Remember, one year honey, and then I can spend a little more time with you," said Lesley as he walked over to the bed and gave her a soft kiss on the cheek, and then strolled out of the room and out the door.

About an hour later, a soft tap whispered from the door, and a shameful smile eased across Laura's face as she walked towards the front door to allow the ending of her dried up, things filled, marriage to helplessly be defiled by a craving that was deeper than herself-a craving that her husband had long neglected and long forgotten.

God's Drops

Where nobody's at
And everybody is
Where learning is void
And everything is known
Where there are no ups or downs
Or ins or outs
But everything is just is

Where God wipes his brow and toss
His sweat upon the grown
And up comes life from the savoring sweat of God
We be but little drops of Him
Drops that evaporate and goes back to him

The trees that reaches so ever to the sky
And the flowers full of sweet nectar with the honey bees
Are but parts of Him
All parts of Him

I am that I am
Because I know Him and fail to know Him
I breathe life into everything around me
Yet I cannot contain life within me
For it daily seeps from me
From me

I have been everywhere
And have been nowhere
I see everything
But I am blinded by nothing

Akeam Simmons

God is the first
And He is the last
He is the beginning and the ending
And all the lively parts that make the whole

I am but His yesterday
He is always my tomorrow
My every moment
My breath of life's living

I KNEW THE LOVE OF GOD
BEFORE I KNEW THE GOD OF LOVE

But Me

Oh that I might find myself amidst
my clutter of racing thoughts
Thoughts of me
The other me
The old me
The new me
But me

Oh when shall I be but free to just be happy with me
All of me
My failures
My issues
My successes
But still me

But me
The real me
That hides from the world
And fights the sky
And envy the stars
But me

I search everywhere trying to find but me
Amongst the learned
Amongst the dumb
Amongst the idiot
Amongst the fool
Amongst the wise
But still no but me

When I close my eyes
I don't see me
I see he that the world wants me to be
I be a stranger to myself
For I have forgotten me
When all the layers all gone and there be but me

My bones be weary from this constant
theatrical stage I perform
Daily I am the leading act
The villain
And hardly ever the hero
But still there is no me

They weaned me to be somebody else
To not be happy with just me
My curly hair
My brown eyes
My wide spread nose
My full lips

Can I just be me
But me
The me they refuse to see
The me they don't want to see

But me
They look beyond and refuse to see
But me
They put a label on me and expect me to be
But me
I have a brain that is uniquely as can be
Just test me and you will see
I am as precious as can be

I just must find me
Without all the clutter that you see
The me
That God made me to be

I shall forever remember August 31, 2013, at 1045 pm; it was then that I leaned over Mama, and watched her take her last breath. I thank God that he allowed me to be there for her last breath, for she was there for my first breath. I don't know if I shall ever see her again on the other side, but I cherish the time she gave to help me become a man . . . . I still remember hearing her prayers for me when I was wild and foolish like many a young boys. She'd pray all the time, "Lord let me live to see my boy get grown." God answered her prayer. Thank God for a praying Mama!

Good night sweet Mama; rest in peace.

The Grave

Every day I pass by the yard
Where all my friends and loved ones be gone
And my enemies go there too
All never return

I peer over into the silent manicured lawn
Where cemented and marbled stone
shoot up from the grown
Claiming who their standing on
And withering leaning flowers shout nobody's home

Everyone says it's a better place
But how do they know or how am I to know
No one has come back and said such was so
But I guess it is how we comfort ourselves of such

Death be so cruel and unforgiving
For it comes for all that's counted among the living
The rich the poor the young the old the sick the healthy
All that's counted among the living will soon die

Thus all is vanity
We go to work to die
We live right to die
We save and invest our money to die
We fall in love to die
We burn with hate to die

We all but die
There is none that will escape
We all but die and go to the yard
Where we hold up cement and marble stones
Telling passer Byers who we once were
And silently warn them of their own soon fate
And where their new address shall soon be
In the yard

Where Flowers Grow

I long to see you again
For the first is but yesterday
For I've held you in my arms a many a times before
But never held you at all

I do taste the sweetness of your lips
As your breaths caress the contours of my melting face
The softness of your touch carries me away
To places I can't even fathom the strength to imagine

Oh but you are the one that dwells where flowers grow
Flowers that can not be plunked
Or cut or hued down
That fragrance the air
And color the sun

My forever budding flower
That renews my strength every day
And causes my youth to race upon me
And carry me places I but can dream

You where flowers grow
Where honey drips from your pebbles
And sweeten the grown below
Where new flowers bud beneath your every step

Would every man had chance to visit where flowers grow
For the world would be filled with laughter
And haughty growth

There every man would long to sleep
For only there is where flowers truly grow
where men and women retain their youth again
and never are burden by yester years harnesses

The footsteps of God
Always grace where flowers grow
He breathe upon them his elegant grace
And causes them to blossom like an early morning sun rise

Oh that I might hide myself
Or at least my heart
In that place where flowers grow

A Prayer

Oh Lord my God
The One that created the heavens and the earth
And everything that be there in and there on
We exalt your name and give you all
the praise and all the glory
For you are worthy to be praised
That you for all of the many blessing
that you have bestowed on us
For if we had a million tongues we
couldn't thank you enough

Now grant us the strength to be able to
withstand and walk through
Our daily storms and our daily victories
and our daily triumphs
And give us a mind to know that it is all in you
Let us not become so defeated until we lose our drive
Or so victorious and filled with triumph until we con not see

Lord order my steps that I might always be close to you
Not so close that you see all of me
And not so for that you see none of me
But enough that you might forgive me and all of my faults
And renew me day by day

Amen